Everyman, I will go with thee,
and be thy guide

THE EVERYMAN
LIBRARY

*The Everyman Library was founded by J. M. Dent in
1906. He chose the name Everyman because he wanted
to make available the best books ever written in every
field to the greatest number of people at the cheapest possible
price. He began with Boswell's 'Life of Johnson';
his one thousandth title was Aristotle's 'Metaphysics', by
which time sales exceeded forty million.*

*Today Everyman paperbacks remain true to
J. M. Dent's aims and high standards, with a wide range
of titles at affordable prices in editions which address
the needs of today's readers. Each new text is reset to give
a clear, elegant page and to incorporate the latest thinking
and scholarship. Each book carries the pilgrim logo,
the character in 'Everyman', a medieval mystery play,
a proud link between Everyman
past and present.*

Dylan Thomas

SELECTED POEMS

Edited with an Introduction and Notes by
WALFORD DAVIES

EVERYMAN
J.M. DENT • LONDON

Copyright © 1934, 1937, 1938, 1941, 1945, 1955, 1956,
1962, 1965, 1966, 1967, 1971

Selected Poems first published with introduction and notes by
Walford Davies in 1974 by Walford Davies
Reprinted 1975, 1977, 1983, 1985, 1988, 1989, 1997, 1998

© New introduction and updated notes Walford Davies 1993

Made in Great Britain by
The Guernsey Press Co. Ltd, Guernsey, C.I.

J. M. Dent
Orion Publishing Group
Orion House
5 Upper St Martin's Lane, London WC2H 9EA

British Library Cataloguing in Publication Data
is available

ISBN 0 460 87298 2

CONTENTS

NOTE ON THE AUTHOR
AND EDITOR

Dylan Marlais Thomas was born in Swansea in 1914. After leaving school he worked briefly as a junior reporter on the *South Wales Evening Post* before embarking on a literary career in London. Here he rapidly established himself as one of the finest poets of his generation. *18 Poems* appeared in 1934, *Twenty-five Poems* in 1936, and *Deaths and Entrances* in 1946; his *Collected Poems* was published in 1952. Throughout his life Thomas wrote short stories, his most famous collection being *Portrait of the Artist as a Young Dog*. He also wrote film-scripts, broadcast stories and talks, lectured in America, and wrote the radio play *Under Milk Wood*. In 1953, shortly after his thirty-ninth birthday, he collapsed and died in New York. His body is buried in Laugharne, Wales, his home for many years.

Walford Davies, from 1976 to 1997 Director of the Department of Continuing Education of the University of Wales, Aberystwyth, is holder of a personal chair in English Literature at the University of Wales. He is the author of two critical studies of the work of Dylan Thomas (*Dylan Thomas*, Open University Press 1986, and *Dylan Thomas*, University of Wales Press 1990). Amongst other volumes, he has edited (for Dent, unless otherwise stated): *Dylan Thomas: Early Prose Writings* (1971), *New Critical Essays* (1972), *Wordsworth: Selected Poems* (1974), *Gerard Manley Hopkins: The Major Poems* (1979), *Thomas Hardy Selected Poems* (1982), *Deaths and Entrances* (Gregynog Press, 1984) and, with Ralph Maud, *Dylan Thomas: Collected Poems 1934-1953* (1988) and *Under Milk Wood* (1995). He is currently writing the authorised biography of R.S. Thomas.

for Jason and Damian,
young and easy

INTRODUCTION

I

But, to start with, if one view makes a bit of poetry very good, and another makes it very bad, the author's intention is inherently likely to be the one that makes it good; especially if we know that he writes well sometimes. We could not use language as we do, and above all we could not learn it when babies, unless we were always floating in a general willingness to make sense of it; all the more, then, to try to make a printed page mean something good is only fair.

(William Empson, *Milton's God*)

A comment by William Empson is an appropriate place to start. His *Seven Types of Ambiguity* (1930) was seminal in shaping critical response to complexity in poetry, and Empson will in fact be a point of reference in many other ways throughout this Introduction. But my first reference is to *Milton's God*. It is a reminder of one of the century's major literary arguments – that regarding the quality and standing of Milton's poetry. Instigated in the 1930s, the debate created strange bed-fellows, with for example C.S. Lewis and Empson ranged against T.S. Eliot and F.R. Leavis. But C.S. Lewis noted an even stranger fact. 'It is not', he said, 'that [Leavis] and I see different things when we look at *Paradise Lost*. He sees and hates the very same that I see and love.'

The most obvious feature of Dylan Thomas's reputation, too, has been the stunning critical disagreement regarding his achievement. And here again the split is often over features quite accurately seen by both sides. The poetry's hard craft and musicality, for example. Or the nature of its main themes. Alastair Fowler felt that he should regard Geoffrey Grigson's dispraise of *Deaths and Entrances* ('not meditation, but simply obsession; – obsession with birth, death, and love') as 'unmeant praise. For obsession with what matters so much may amount to intense seriousness'. But the debate has sometimes verged on gang-warfare, in which unrecognisable things are seen and claimed. Even Empson on

Milton (in a 1958 letter to the *T.L.S.*) had to utter a cry of blank frustration: 'I can sympathize with a critic who feels he cannot take seriously a proof that [*Paradise Lost*] is bad – it is so evidently not bad'. But criticism is a case of begging, not agreeing, to differ, and for that reason I shall use the negative side of the Thomas debate as a platform for discussion.

The argument has been peculiar in the range of emotion and energy it has aroused, and empty claims and lunatic explanations have been as prominent on the favourable side as silly insults and stubborn prejudice have been on the other. The pity is that voices either side of the argument have been most memorable when they have been most extreme. Edith Sitwell's kind but always nebulous advocacy of Thomas's talents from the early 1930s, or Philip Toynbee's tactless claim in reviewing the *Collected Poems* in 1952 that Thomas was 'the greatest living poet in the English language', are unfortunately better known even today than T.S. Eliot's quiet remark, 'I certainly regarded him always as a poet of considerable importance'. Similarly, books which make ridiculous claims for a structured erudition on Thomas's part in fields such as Greek myth and astronomy (Elder Olson) or Egyptian funerary customs and marine biology (H.H. Kleinman) have not only stimulated a backlash but also obscured the subtlety with which an already impressive range of knowledge and reading feeds into the work. Over-extended claims have diluted the effect of more soberly championing examinations in books by Ralph Maud or William T. Moynihan, or in essays by William Empson, J. Hillis Miller, or John Wain.

From the start a need has been understandably felt to correct fulsome praise. But it has also led to a great deal of over-compensating. Thomas's most strident opponents often ignore a fact as basic to literary criticism as it is to law: that you won't get even a conviction for theft on a charge of murder. In his Clark Lectures at Cambridge, published as *The Crowning Privilege* in 1955, Robert Graves did not claim that Thomas's 'If my head hurt a hair's foot' (1939) was difficult or that it was not to his taste; he simply said that it made no sense at all. (Indeed, Graves bet a pound note on the fact, but refused to pay when M.J.C. Hodgart produced a perfectly clear account of the poem.) Or there's the case of the *Scrutiny* critics. They simply assumed that the principles implied in their excellent treatment of classic poets spoke volumes in the gaps of what was a very scrappy and insulting treatment of Thomas, as indeed of contemporary poetry as a whole. Where Thomas was concerned, the Scrutineers spared only a glance. Their treatment of him was a victory of tone rather than of demonstration, a fact reflected even in the final Index to the complete series of the magazine, where Thomas figures under such gauchely legislative headings as 'failure to mature', 'repudiated by critics with high standards' and 'mythology dismissed'. Similarly, when Donald Davie in *Articulate Energy* (1955) and George Steiner in *Language and Silence* (1967) levelled their respective accusations of 'pseudo syntax' and 'imposter', they somehow felt it fair to do so in a mere passing reference, and to share no more than one (mis)quotation between them. In contrast, David Holbrook looked long and hard, in two complete studies, but only to find that Dylan Thomas, apparently, was psychologically damaged at source. Holbrook, very much concerned with the kind of *person* he thinks Thomas to have been, fails to make the necessary division between (in Eliot's phrase) 'the man who suffers and the mind which creates', or (in W.B. Yeats's racier image) between the poet who writes the poem and 'the bundle of accident and incoherence that sits down to breakfast'.

II

Overkill is apparent in many areas of the anti-Thomas faction. A representative example is the case of Geoffrey Grigson, a critic normally of real discrimination, whether as Editor of *New Verse*, the most influential poetry magazine of the 1930s, or as a critic of even unorthodox poets such as Gerard Manley Hopkins. Early on, Grigson was a friend of Thomas's, both in the personal sense and in that between 1934 and 1937 he published nine of Thomas's poems, plus some reviews and other contributions in *New Verse*. In his book *The Harp of Aeolus* (1948), however, Grigson unleashed a bitter attack on Thomas's poetry. In its general principles, the essay validly reaffirms Hopkins's warnings about 'frigidities' and 'untruths to nature' in poetic imagery. But what is disconcerting, indeed insulting, is the *way* in which Grigson applies his principles to the case of Dylan Thomas. One could demonstrate Grigson's clear prejudice against Thomas's use of half-rhymes, his rhythms, or the poetry's central concern with the human body. But I shall content myself with the following example.

In the middle of Grigson's essay, we find this:

No more, no less construable is:

> There was a saviour
> In the churches of his tears
> There was calm to be done in his safe unrest
> Children kept from the sun
> On to the ground when a man has died
> To hear the golden note turn in a groove,
> Silence, silence to do, when earth grew loud
> In the jails and studies of his keyless smiles.

– a stanza upon which Mr Thomas's explorers and admirers should meditate, for reasons which I shall give later.

Over the page, Grigson returns to cock a snook at anyone who has in the meantime been admiring the quoted lines. The stanza, you see, is bogus. Grigson simply put together eight completely unrelated lines from 'There was a saviour' (1940), claiming triumphantly if oddly to have sprung a successful trap – because, as he says over the page, 'it reads, I am convinced, as authentically as most of Mr Thomas's stanzas'. One wonders what sort of helpless audience Grigson had in mind whom he could expect either to fall into the trap and blush from embarrassment, or wink in approval at such a ploy. But quite apart from the cheapness of the trick, and the fact that Grigson's fifth line is a damaging misquotation, let us consider the claim which the deceit was designed to serve.

The obvious thing to do is to quote a genuine stanza from Thomas's poem, to stand against Grigson's cynical mock-up:

> There was a saviour
> Rarer than radium,
> Commoner than water, crueller than truth;
> Children kept from the sun
> Assembled at his tongue
> To hear the golden note turn in a groove,
> Prisoners of wishes locked their eyes
> In the jails and studies of his keyless smiles.

A fundamental difference is clear. The authentic stanza has in the first place a rhythmic convincingness – the music of phrases and lines and the rhythmic backbone which makes Thomas's stanza a pliant unit. The Grigson forgery is rhythmically inert. If it was an accusation of inertness that he wished to make, he would have done more honestly to try and argue from fact than fiction – indeed, to try and argue in the first place. And if the accusation was meant to be one of emptiness of meaning, then fact again ruins his fiction. For while Grigson's jumbled lines add up to nothing (despite his amazing claim that they are 'just-construable'!), Thomas's actual stanza gets down to real work. It establishes a point of departure by evoking the historical Christ, and initiates the poem's Blakean argument that Christ's message has been corrupted by organised religion into selfish wish-fulfilment and arid debate. Of course, that abstract does not do justice to the wit of the actual poetry. The way, for example, this evocation of the early church is tinged with the poet's own early memories of Sunday-school or school assembly, where 'children kept from the sun/ Assembled . . . To hear the golden note' of the message produced by rote. The theme is people's tendency to make restrictive ('jails and studies') that which was itself open ('keyless').

From here the poem also develops to be a powerful war poem, an indictment of the abandonment of individual moral responsi-bility for an escapist 'Christian' piety. The image of 'children kept from the sun' also nicely inverts the phrase 'Children of the Sun' used of the self-publicising aesthetes who dominated English cultural life in the 1920s and 1930s. What is more, by quoting the lines as Thomas actually wrote them, we see how he makes his form comment on his meaning because, for this confrontation with historical Christianity, Thomas has ironically borrowed the stanza-form of Milton's Hymn, 'On the Morning of Christ's Nativity', which Kathleen Raine recorded was Thomas's favour-ite poem. Did Grigson recognise the stylistic allusion, and choose to vandalise it; or did he just not recognise it? 'There was a Saviour' is most certainly not the lifeless sham that Grigson's piece of glum sabotage would have us believe.

The case of Geoffrey Grigson (that of Stephen Spender would be another) exemplifies a contemporary hostility that existed side by side with increasing popular acclaim, widened beyond narrow academic taste by Thomas's gradual emergence also as the writer of excellent comic prose, inventive broadcaster, film writer and lecturer. A new reader can look this Grigsonian period hostility straight in the face, but he will do so more steadily if he has first 'heard' the poetry's authentic voice for himself. This will alert him to some weird misrepresentations in today's criticism, too. For example, a critic recently argued that the following parody shows how easily imitated Thomas is – that 'many of the worst trade-marks of Thomas's poetry are here: the distinctive syllabic patterns, grammatical deviation, refrains, sound allusions, even – similar emotions':

> When we were too young in our happiness,
> Knowing only the sun that kissed our world
> And peeled our sand-streaked backs;
> Yet we were blind to see our unknown lives
> Went spinning through our apple-born faces.
> We, who sang our sad song all long summer long;
> Yet we were blind how in our gilded voices
> We sang our sad song to the lukewarm wind.

It isn't clear why the characteristics listed (even 'grammatical deviation', and most certainly 'refrains') should be considered faults in the first place. In any case they do not function here in anything resembling Dylan Thomas's manner. In fact, a 'syllabic pattern' (of which Thomas was indeed fond) cannot come into being until it is repeated; in the meantime the above parody can only be called free verse. The 'grammatical deviation' that leaves the adverbial clauses of the first three lines, and the sixth, sus-pended in limbo without a main verb is in fact illiterate and is not matched in any poem Thomas ever published. It's not that one wants, in William Empson's phrase, to slip in some main verbs 'like ferrets'; it's just that if 'when' in the first line and 'who' in the sixth are removed, correct grammar returns with a click – showing how superficially sabotaged it was in the first place. 'Grammatical deviation' should be more creatively subversive than that. Anyway, the nullity of the rhythm and the banality of the wording ('unknown lives', 'we were blind', 'our sad song', 'the lukewarm wind') are debilities that no mere tricks could sting awake.

The specific Thomas poem that made this alleged 'ease of imitation' seem possible – 'Fern Hill' (1945) – is nowhere even remotely hit off. Here, for example, is 'Fern Hill's' final stanza:

> Nothing I cared, in the lamb white days, that time would take me
> Up to the swallow thronged loft by the shadow of my hand,

In the moon that is always rising,
        Nor that riding to sleep
    I should hear him fly with the high fields
And wake to the farm forever fled from the childless land.
Oh as I was young and easy in the mercy of his means,
            Time held me green and dying
        Though I sang in my chains like the sea.

Talking of 'sound allusions', where in the parody is there any-
thing like those subtle end-of-line assonances ('rising' . . . 'high
fields' . . . 'dying') or that beautifully judged internal rhyme of
'rising' with 'riding' – effects that haunt us without halting us?
A syntax that moves forward in this way by constantly gathering,
recouping and husbanding itself complements the remembrance
of things past in 'Fern Hill', and involves an inwardness with
language that is nowhere even signposted in the parody. But the
parody's striking unlikeness to a poem like 'Fern Hill' (despite
what are optimistically claimed to be 'similar emotions') is not
the point. The truth is that it does not sound like any Dylan
Thomas at all.

    This matters because (to quote Thomas's 'To Others than You',
1939) a lie can 'displace a truth in the air'. Like misquotations,
versions of poems too often replace poems. To sharpen our respect
for the authentic, A.E. Housman even urged us to imagine a
literal displacement, to imagine that 'the book of poems had
perished and the verse survived only in the review . . .' The same
applies to misrepresentations of a poet's personal life. In the forty
years since Thomas's death in 1953, every kind of capital has been
made trading in travesties. A readiness to hold forth on the untidy
life without any consideration of the meticulous art it produced
coexists in some commentators with rank disapproval of anyone
who would detach the art in the same way. The very repetitiveness
with which some have run down the man is intriguing – with no
'on the other hand' about it at all. Kingsley Amis, for example,
has woven his hatred of Thomas into review, essay, poem and
novel form, with a strange energy. One does not have to like the
poetry to wonder why Thomas's *good* personal qualities (pro-
found moral outrage at the obscenity of war, for example, or the
total absence of cynicism or clubbable snobbery of any kind) are
never judged to have influenced it. There seems something unique
about the exact chemistry of Thomas's reputation that aggravates
disproportionate animus where it occurs. Racial, cultural and

class tremors are palpably involved, combined possibly with residual envy of the poet's apparently effortless conquering of lucrative America. Certainly, the drunkenness and the scrounging cannot explain it all. Facts morally far more intolerable are known about other poets (blatant racism, for example, or an obsession with pornography, or personal cruelty) but *they* don't get interposed between poem and reader by these detractors. No art is totally divorceable from the artist. It manifests his native ground, his reflexes and assumptions just as surely as his ideas, and part of art's very meaning is what it challenges or depresses, delights or exposes in others. In a Britain too often interchangeably called 'England', art that stems from the 'regions' is what reminds us that 'the isle is full of noises . . . that give delight and hurt not'– if heard with some humility. But a *national* otherness is not just 'regional'. And there is so much in Thomas that cannot be divorced from his very Welshness – let alone his anti-intellectualism, his provincialism, or the surprisingly young age out of which most of the poems came – that his Welshness might well be the catalyst in this negative 'chemistry'. But prejudice against *any* of these is not a good starting-point. On the simpler matter of personal weaknesses, perhaps the recent *Selected Letters* and biography of Philip Larkin, creating as they have an appetite for documenting others of that immediate post-Thomas generation, will redress the balance by bringing into perspective a wider range of writers needing reminders about motes and beams. In the meantime, something Gabriel Pearson wrote about Thomas over twenty years ago still needs to be praised for its judiciousness. 'The legend', he said, 'is still an un-negotiated legacy, fraught with predictable discomfort however you play it, whether with aloofness or bold enthusiasm. Either way, Thomas remains powerful, disreputable and not to be patronised.'

III

In the 1930s and 1940s much of the opposition to Thomas's poetry involved associating it with Surrealism and with 'New Romantic' and 'New Apocalypse' poetry. As far as Surrealism is concerned, it is important to stress that few poets deserve less the charge of 'automatic writing' than Thomas. The twenty-one year old poet felt genuinely insulted when Richard Church hinted such a charge in a letter of 1935:

> I think I do know what some of the main faults of my writing are: immature violence, rhythmic monotony, frequent muddleheadedness, and a very much overweighted imagery that leads too often to incoherence. But every line *is* meant to be understood; the reader *is* meant to understand every poem by thinking and feeling about it, not by sucking it in through his pores, or whatever he is meant to do with surrealist writing.

He had no time at all for the work of the English Surrealist poets of the 1930s – that of David Gascoyne, for example, who spoke approvingly of 'a perpetual flow of irrational thought in the form of images' – and Thomas would in any case have mistrusted the degree to which Surrealism had already been politicised before it reached England in 1936. In that year, as a provincial young man fascinated by the weird fashions of London artistic society in that decade, he certainly turned up at the International Surrealist Exhibition in the New Burlington Galleries, joining in the fun by passing around cups of boiled string, asking 'Weak or strong?' And at a deeper level, it is clear that Surrealism fruitfully tinged the imagination of many poets – early Eliot, for example – who cannot be meaningfully labelled 'Surrealist'. Springing out of the perhaps more gleeful Dadaism of First World War France (and to some degree a way of stressing, by outdoing, the meaninglessness of that war) Surrealism was, like Freudianism, a tincture that was difficult to avoid. Thomas's own shaping happened very much in that phase of the inter-war period that followed the first number of the *Surrealist Revolution* in 1924 and the founding in 1927 of the Surrealist, Paris-based magazine, *transition*, in which he published a poem and a short story in 1936. But when, during the Second World War, he writes in 'On a Wedding Anniversary' (1945) that 'From every true or crater/ Carrying cloud, Death strikes their house' is Grigson right in sneering that 'Clouds with craters are like veins with ears', that the words 'are nearly automatic'? Given that the poem is obviously about death in one of the air-raids, what is wrong with the image's obvious meaning: that the cloud-like formation of dropping bombs will produce a crater where they land? When Grigson includes in this charge of 'automatic' writing the moving and authoritative 'A Refusal to Mourn the Death, by Fire, of a Child in London' (1945) one begins to wonder whether one is even reading the same poem.

But let us take a more testing case, the opening of a much more difficult, early poem:

> When, like a running grave, time tracks you down,
> Your calm and cuddled is a scythe of hairs,
> Love in her gear is slowly through the house,
> Up naked stairs, a turtle in a hearse,
> Hauled to the dome,
>
> Comes, like a scissors stalking, tailor age ...

At the time, Thomas considered 'When, like a running grave' one of the two best poems in his first collection, *18 Poems* (1934), so it is not likely to have been a trivial piece of 'automatic' writing. Yet a 'running grave', a 'scythe of hairs' and a 'turtle in a hearse' certainly look 'surrealistic'. But they are clearly not the product of accident. The connections between such images have been very consciously achieved. For example, time as 'a running grave' later yields an image of a cinder track, just as later images of disease give 'running' here the sense of suppuration, as in a 'running' sore. The 'scythe of hairs', a quite traditional image of grim reaping, is one that scythes hairs. More exciting is the way 'is' in the third line is made first to look like a complete verb, a positive invading presence – 'Love in her gear *is* slowly through the house . . .' It is dramatic therefore when it turns out to be only part of a verb in a passive action: '*is . . . hauled* to the dome [of the head]'. The image is that of man's intellectualisation of love under the threat of time. These carefully planned dualities continue with 'gear' which is both mechanical (because of 'hearse') and (because of 'tailor') an image of clothes, as in *night-gear*. The idea of clothes then prompts the witty description of uncarpeted stairs as 'naked'. The 'turtle', the traditional love-symbol, is a *turtle-dove*, but not without also suggesting a literal turtle – the slowest animal, therefore, in the slowest vehicle ('hearse').

The difficulty in these earlier poems obviously comes from a crush, not an absence, of meanings, and the wit with which the connections are made is highly characteristic of the poetry at all stages. The charge of 'automatic writing' is in any case refuted by the evidence of Thomas's notebooks and manuscript work-sheets, and of his correspondence with Vernon Watkins from 1936 onwards. These show us a painfully conscious craftsman at work. Thomas was therefore justified in feeling aggrieved at Stephen

Spender's charge (in a review of *Twenty-five Poems* in the Communist *Daily Worker* in 1936) that his poetry 'is turned on like a tap; it is just poetic stuff with no beginning nor end, shape, or intelligent and intelligible control'. With modest matter-of-factness Thomas rejoined:

> Spender's remark is really the exact opposite of what is true. My poems *are* formed; they are not turned on like a tap at all, they are 'watertight compartments'. Much of the obscurity is due to rigorous compression; the last thing they do is to flow; they are much rather hewn. Now Spender himself has no idea of form; his poetry is so much like poetry, & so remote from poems, that I think most of his work will become almost as unreadable as the worst of the Georgians – & very soon.

Grigson's view was expressed significantly later. In 1947, when his essay was first published (in *Polemic*), he was more pointedly associating Thomas with the 'New Romanticism' of the 1940s. The title of Grigson's essay – 'How Much Me Now Your Acrobatics Amaze' – was in fact a line from a poem by George Barker. 'New Romantic' poets such as Barker, W.S. Graham, and W.R. Rodgers, along with the 'New Apocalypse' poets led by Henry Treece and J.F. Hendry (and edited by them in three wartime anthologies) clearly recognised in Thomas a meaningful alternative to the more intellectual and politically committed talents of the poets grouped by reputation around W.H. Auden. But Thomas cannot be held responsible for any limitations these poets, too, might be thought to have; he saw himself as no part, let alone the leader, of any movement whatsoever. Paradoxically, perhaps Grigson did less disservice to Thomas than is done nowadays by those who more vaguely claim that he was simply 'the best of that group'. That is exactly the force of Gabriel Pearson's warning, that Thomas is not to be patronised.

The 1940s were nevertheless Thomas's decade. In the 1930s there had been felt, for one thing, the dwarfing presence of the century's two greatest poets, Yeats and Eliot. Yeats was then drawing to the end of his magnificent career, but his *New Poems* (1938) and his posthumous *Last Poems* (1939) stood strongly at the end of that decade. Eliot, whose *Collected Poems* appeared in 1936, was very much the on-going genius, with *Four Quartets* as such still to come when the decade closed. But since a generation tends to identify with its younger contemporaries, the real signature stamped on the 1930s had been that of Auden. In the 1940s, however, with Yeats dead, with *Four Quartets* bringing Eliot's poetry to an obvious fulness in 1944, and with Auden in America, hindsight probably allowed some to feel that the 1930s had in reality been shared by Auden and Thomas together. This is certainly how it looks from today's distance. Thomas's emphasis on the elemental and the emotive, and Auden's on the intellectual and the detached now seem the complementary halves that Yeats ('blood, intellect, imagination running together') and Eliot ('A thought to Donne was an experience; it modified his sensibility') had sought to fuse. And no doubt it was social and cultural conditioning that caused English Auden's intellectualism and Welsh Thomas's emotiveness each to undervalue the other.

Either way, as the 1940s wore on, Thomas came more and more into his own. It was the publication of his fourth volume, *Deaths and Entrances* in 1946, including as it did more immediately approachable poems like 'Poem in October', 'A Refusal to Mourn', 'The hunchback in the park' and 'Fern Hill', that gave Thomas his real and unignorable position, helped as it was also by his comic autobiography in short stories, *Portrait of the Artist as a Young Dog* (1940) and his increasing popularity as a broadcaster. His fame continued into the 1950s, until his tragically early death on a lecture-tour in America in 1953. In 1952, his *Collected Poems* had set his achievement in front of all interested parties, friends and enemies alike. At one moment he had looked like a natural survivor; in another, he had done the unforgivable thing – gone out with a bang.

IV

The sense of climax, and the large-scale sense of shock which greeted his death, focused uncompromisingly the degree and nature of his celebrity. It was a natural moment for the now legendary irresponsibilities of the life to be felt, not necessarily vindictively, as a freewheeling lack of discipline also affecting his verse. The most meaningful sign of that view is the reaction implicit in the preoccupations and techniques of the new generation of poets who emerged in the 1950s. Any new reader approaching Dylan Thomas's poetry today does so in a literary atmosphere initiated and still influenced by that generation. The poets involved – Philip Larkin, Donald Davie, John Wain, Kingsley

Amis, Thom Gunn, for example – were given some kind of unified weight, despite their differences, by their collection into an anthology called *New Lines*, edited by Robert Conquest in 1956. (Another *New Lines* anthology came out in 1963.) As early as 1954, the group had been hallowed by a journalistic title – 'The Movement'. By no means did all the poets involved think Thomas negligible. But the very assumptions of their own work – control of emotion, understatement, sober diction – were reversals of Thomas's emotional expansiveness, his rhetoric, and verbal inventiveness.

In this sense it was revisionism, not revolution. Unlike a Donne, a Wordsworth or a T.S. Eliot, whose revolutions lay in querying literary decorum in the choice of poetic language, genres and form, the poets of the 1950s were *reimposing* decorum. At the same time they were re-intellectualising the world of poetry, superannuating any 'Romantic' or 'Bardic' concept of the poet. And there can be no doubt today that English poetry has gained from their chastening efforts. Where reaction to Thomas springs in this way from new creative needs, that reaction is already beyond the area of in-fighting, of rights and wrongs, or of vengeful value-judgements. In contrast, those detractors who were Thomas's actual contemporaries, like Geoffrey Grigson or Stephen Spender, often sound merely as if they thought it too early to have another successful poet who relied so little on what Eliot, or especially Auden, could teach him.

In a 'Postscript 1966' to his brilliant critical book *Purity of Diction in English Verse* (1952), Donald Davie shows how the book's treatment of poetic diction in late Eighteenth Century poetry was almost a manifesto for the Movement poets, and significantly adds that much of it was 'a reaction from the tawdry amoralism of a London Bohemia which had destroyed Dylan Thomas, the greatest talent of the generation before ours'. It is the way it springs from Davie's personal concerns as a poet that saves that description from being simple condescension. For Davie, part of any poet's quality depends on what his work is able to hand on to later poets, in a broad tradition dictated by a general agreement on 'the nature of English as a spoken and written language'. In a chapter in *Purity of Diction in English Verse* entitled 'Hopkins as a Decadent Critic' it is the basic principles implicit in Hopkins's heterodox poetry, as they might influence others, that are taken to task. There is real force in this view;

Hopkins and Thomas are notoriously dangerous poets to copy unthinkingly. This is where the Milton debate comes back to mind. The explanation behind T.S. Eliot's dislike of Milton was the one already expressed a century earlier by Keats: 'I have but lately stood on my guard against Milton. Life to him would be death to me.' But even so, does non-transferability diminish poets in themselves? Isn't that a matter, not for criticism, but for literary history? Mightn't Donald Davie 'praise and go and do otherwise'? Certainly it is an irony that the poet of the 1930s whose work most influenced the style and intellectualism of the Movement – William Empson – was himself a profound admirer of both Dylan Thomas and Hopkins.

At the same time, Empson's caveat about the poetry of the 1950s – that it too often lacked what he called 'the root of the matter . . . a singing line' – matches G.S. Fraser's point when he applied to the Movement poets Roy Campbell's famous rebuke:

> You praise the firm restraint with which they write –
> I'm with you there, of course:
> They use the snaffle and the curb all right,
> But where's the bloody horse?

Of course, this is not to say that the Movement poets were not awake to dangers in their own position. Donald Davie's 'Remembering the Thirties', a poem demythologising the poetic and political 'heroism' of the 1930s, also acknowledged the risk of jettisoning impressiveness *with* absurdity:

> A neutral tone is nowadays preferred.
> And yet it may be better, if we must,
> To find the stance impressive and absurd
> Than not to see the hero for the dust.

That allusion to Thomas Hardy's 'Neutral Tones' brings in another major poetic influence on the 1950s. The fact that Hardy was at the same time Dylan Thomas's favourite modern shows the rich and often contradictory heritage from which the Movement poets sought to find their bearings. A new reader, perhaps approaching Dylan Thomas for the first time in this selection, has a refreshing freedom that comes with greater distance. Also adding objectivity is the fact that the last three decades have in any case seen reactions also to the Movement, reactions to a reaction. Reading A. Alvarez's anthology, *The New*

Poetry (Penguin, revised edition 1966), is a good way of seeing how quickly the sobering aims of the Movement were themselves reacted against. Alvarez sought a poetry that went 'beyond the gentility principle' and that registered the implicit psychological disturbance of an age that had after all seen two world wars, the concentration camps, genocide, and the threat of nuclear war. He placed considerable emphasis on the work of Sylvia Plath and Ted Hughes, both of whom were creatively indebted to Dylan Thomas. For Alvarez, 'Thomas was not only a fine rhetorician, he also, in his early poems, had something rather original to say'. This notable emphasis on meaning was exactly the balance that needed redressing. Of course, *The New Poetry*, no less than the *New Lines* anthologies, made its 'alternative' grouping seem tidier than it was (it had in any case to include many of the Movement poets themselves). But what such groupings do is keep current those expectations left unsatisfied by dominant fashion at any time. As it happens, it is only now being realised how much Dylan Thomas himself satisfies Alvarez's requirement that a poet's language should register (without necessarily talking about) the psychological tremors of its age. The Audenesque poem about tyranny, 'The hand that signed the paper' (1933), may be Thomas's only overtly political poem. But, born like the First World War in 1914, in 'I dreamed my genesis' (1934) he placed that war's atrocities at the very heart of his autobiography:

> I dreamed my genesis and died again, shrapnel
> Rammed in the marching heart, hole
> In the stitched wound and clotted wind, muzzled
> Death on the mouth that ate the gas.

But *The New Poetry* also kept open an appetite for textural, not just topical, energy – a respect for poetry that is strongly worded. And that, in turn, kept open a line linking Thomas via Ted Hughes and Sylvia Plath to Geoffrey Hill and Seamus Heaney.

V

I should like now to select one of Dylan Thomas's early poems and give some account of it, as a guide to how he can be approached. On the whole, new readers will probably find the later poems more accessible. I select an early poem because it was at this period (from 1930 to 1934, when Thomas was between sixteen and twenty years of age) that he was first discovering an independent voice in poetry, and his main qualities are best revealed at their most uncompromising. As William Empson put it, 'it is the first inspiration, the poems the young man hit the town with (overwhelmingly good, though one resisted them because one couldn't see why), which are the permanent challenge to a critic.' By grounding my discussion in one poem, I am inviting the reader to test my comments against his own reading. I shall, however, move away from my chosen example as the need arises. My aim is to characterise the main features of Thomas's early style and preoccupations.

The poem is 'I see the boys of summer', written in April 1934 (p. 25). This would have been the first poem the reader would have encountered on opening Dylan Thomas's first published volume, *18 Poems*. In that position, its power and oddness had something of the uncompromising impact that 'The Love Song of J. Alfred Prufrock' had at the prow of T.S. Eliot's first volume in 1917. The first thing to strike us is the absence of a conventional title. It is characteristic of especially an early Thomas poem to make its own opening words serve as title. It suggests a refusal to abstract 'meaning' prematurely, a refusal to forecast a narrative other than the one we are meant to possess only in the reading. Instead of directing our attention to a graspable whole as more conventional titles do, Thomas's early titles (even those of volumes – *18 Poems*, *Twenty-five Poems*) merely warn us that we shall have to start again at the beginning of each poem, and on its own terms. The dramatic effect of such titles is as an invitation – to listen-in to a poem as essentially a narrative event, as can be suggested by some characteristic examples in isolation: 'Especially when the October wind . . .', 'Light breaks where no sun shines . . .', 'If I were tickled by the rub of love . . .'

On reading further we feel that certain concepts, such as fruitfulness and aridity, are communicated before we can gauge or clearly describe what the poem, in the usual sense, is 'about'. We also notice early how such concepts are constantly being set in opposition to each other. In the first line, for example, 'the boys of *summer*' are 'in their *ruin*', the '*gold tithings* are laid *barren*'. The reader is, in fact, already in touch with the poem's main theme, a concern with the dialectics of growth and decay as they underlie our general sense of life. But in my words the theme is a mere abstract; Thomas's actual poem is concrete, its language almost tangible. It also gives us the sense, not only of a general theme, but of an actual situation. After all, it draws our attention to 'These boys of light', and in the final section even addresses them as '*you* boys of summer'. We feel, in other words, that the 'boys of summer' of the first two stanzas are in a real sense boys, however private Thomas's feelings about them may be. In the same way, the 'summer children in their mothers' of the third and fourth stanzas are actual unborn children in the womb.

In a letter of the same month as the poem, Thomas wrote: 'I see the unborn children struggling up the hill in their mothers, beating on the jailing slab of the womb, little realising what a smugger prison they wish to leap into.' By the end of the first section of the poem, the speaker has made a specific accusation: that the boys he sees around him are turning that which is fruitful and life-giving into that which is sour or frozen; and that those children still to be born will grow up to do the same. What Thomas is drawing attention to seem to be codes of conduct which deny natural impulses. We begin to feel that the implied subject of the poem is the kind of society which places restraints on, say, natural sexuality. It seems reasonable to suspect that the immediate Welsh Nonconformist, puritanical society in which he was growing up is in Thomas's mind, a society which encourages 'frigid threads of doubt and dark' (stanza two). In this sense, the area in which the poem works is not all that far from Edward Arlington Robinson's brilliant satire in 'New England':

> Here where the wind is always north-north-east
> And children learn to walk on frozen toes,
> Wonder begets an envy of all those
> Who boil elsewhere with such a lyric yeast
> Of love . . .
>
> Passion is here a soilure of the wits,
> We're told, and Love a cross for them to bear;
> Joy shivers in the corner where she knits
> And Conscience always has the rocking-chair . . .

The sentence from Thomas's letter about the unborn children was part of a wider description of what he could see outside the window of his childhood Swansea home:

Sunday in Wales. The Sunday-walkers have slunk out of the warrens in which they sleep and breed all the unholy week, have put on their

black suits, reddest eyes, & meanest expressions, and are now march-
ing up the hill past my window. Fathers are pointing out the view to
their stiff-collared whelps ... and all the starch, the thin pink blood,
the hot salty longings, and the respectable cream on the top of the
suburban scum, run down the stones, like a river end up in the Sabbath
well where the corpses of strangled preachers, promising all their days
a heaven they don't believe in to people who won't go there, float and
hide truth. Life passes the windows, and I hate it more minute by
minute. I see the rehearsed gestures, the correct smiles, the grey cells
revolving around nothing under the godly bowlers.

In such a society youth is old before its time. The 'boys of summer'
become the 'men of nothing' of stanza four. A Swansea friend
recalls walking with the young Dylan Thomas on the beach at
that time and hearing him call some middle-aged men in Corpo-
ration bathing-suits 'boys of summer in their ruin'. Poems very
often spring from an isolated phrase or image, and the key phrase
here might in turn have been suggested by Auden's analysis of the
sickness of a different society in 'Consider', ('that distant after-
noon . . . They gave the prizes to the ruined boys'), just as
Thomas's poem itself caught the imagination sufficiently to pro-
vide the title (and its first three lines, the epigraph) of the best
book ever written about American baseball, Roger Kahn's *The
Boys of Summer* (1971). Such far-flung imaginative currency is
all the more remarkable when we realise the poem's source in the
social world of a Swansea nineteen-year-old in the early 1930s.
Though this social context is not reflected in realistic detail in the
early poems, we always do well to bear it in mind, along with the
idea of what it feels like to be an adolescent seeking to register the
facts of life, death and sexuality without using the moral language
in which society usually teaches us to think.

Hints as to how the rest of 'I see the boys of summer' develops
will be found in the Notes. Our present, broader aim is to decide
what *kind* of poem it is. In theme it is reminiscent of Blake,
especially the *Songs of Experience* and *The Marriage of Heaven
and Hell*, and of D.H. Lawrence, both of whom greatly preoccu-
pied the young Thomas. In a letter of December 1933, in which
he deals (not uncritically) with Lawrence's teachings, Thomas
writes of 'the philosophy which, declaring the intellect and the
reason and the intelligence to be *all*, denies the warmth of the
blood and the body's promise'. The poem's phallic image of 'poles
of promise' probably comes from some such preoccupations.

Similarly, Blake comes to mind because of his conviction that society suppresses the natural impulses of childhood and replaces physical instinct with abstract morality and reason. And the comparison goes further because, like Thomas, Blake developed a highly personal range of symbols with which to body forth that vision, in poems such as 'The Sick Rose', 'The Garden of Love', 'London', and 'Infant Sorrow'.

But in order to draw out the *stylistic* characteristics of 'I see the boys of summer', let us introduce a very different kind of poem. Here are the first three stanzas of Thomas Hardy's 'To an Unborn Pauper Child':

> Breathe not, hid Heart: cease silently,
> And though thy birth-hour beckons thee,
>   Sleep the long sleep:
>   The Doomsters heap
> Travails and teens around us here,
> And Time-wraiths turn our songsingings to fear.
>
> Hark, how the peoples surge and sigh,
> And laughters fail, and greetings die:
>   Hopes dwindle; yea,
>   Faiths waste away,
> Affections and enthusiasms numb;
> Thou canst not mend these things if thou dost come.
>
> Had I the ear of wombèd souls
> Ere their terrestrial chart unrolls,
>   And thou wert free
>   To cease, or be,
> Then would I tell thee all I know,
> And put it to thee: Wilt thou take Life so?

The comparison is a convenient one because Hardy, too, is concerned with the kind of society the child will be born into, and with the difference between potential and reality. (In a different way, we could also compare Hardy's poem with Thomas's 'If my head hurt a hair's foot'.) But equally convenient are the exaggerated differences between Hardy's and Thomas's use of language. Hardy's language is essentially discursive – one might say 'public' – carrying ideas openly and obviously. We are more aware of the ideas than of the words which carry them (a contrast one would make even with Robinson's 'New England'). One reason for this is Hardy's sequence of abstract words – 'travails', 'teens', 'fear', 'laughters', 'greetings', 'hopes', 'faiths', and so on. It is also clear that Society as such is in the *foreground* of Hardy's poem, and is being obviously 'talked *about*'. As a result, the poem has a directly moral, humane tone. It would not be difficult to give some account of it in paraphrase.

Any paraphrase of 'I see the boys of summer', on the other hand, would be bound to seem a gross simplification of its effects. The first thing to stress is the concreteness of its language, though a better word would be 'literalness'. Images such as 'gold tithings', 'soils', 'winter floods', 'cargoed apples' in the first stanza are not in the ordinary sense metaphors or symbols. That is to say, they do not 'stand for' other things. This is shown by the sheer impossibility (or futility) of finding point-for-point equivalents for them. What Thomas is doing is creating a network of images which replaces the real world, while still expecting us to know what 'soils', 'floods', and 'apples' are. This is exactly what he meant when he insisted, as he so often did, that his early poems should be read 'literally'. When T.S. Eliot was once asked to explain the meaning of his line (from 'Ash Wednesday') 'Lady, three white leopards sat under a juniper-tree', he replied that it meant 'Lady, three white leopards sat under a juniper-tree'. What both Eliot and Thomas were insisting on was the fact that poetry of this kind is irreducible, that its actual language is not there to be unpacked, like some suitcase, of its 'meanings'. Which, of course, is not the same thing as saying that it does not have any meanings, but that they are ideas brought to birth in our minds while reading. They are not presented *as* ideas in the poem. Judgements come into play in something like the way described by Randall Jarrell:

> in poetry you make judgements by your own preliminary choice of symbols, and force the reader who accepts the symbols to accept the judgements implicit in them. A symbol . . . is a nest of judgements; the reader may accept the symbols, and then be cautious about accepting judgements or generalizations, but the damage is done.

Of course, left like that, Jarrell's comment applies to any poetry that does not rely on plain statement, especially if it makes dense use of the independent logic of concrete metaphors. But two developments shaping the history of early twentieth-century poetry had sought to refine that irreducibility further, to the point where a poem could be allowed not to 'mean' but simply to *be*.

One was Imagism, an Anglo-American movement which flour-
ished (very argumentatively) around 1909–15 and which insisted
on the sharp, ordinary literalness of individual images – 'hard
light, clear edges', as Ezra Pound put it. The other phenomenon
was Symbolism, which had its origins in the late nineteenth
century *symboliste* poetry of France. The first major manifesta-
tion of Modernist poetry, Symbolist verse was already, in its
emphasis on poetry as an image-making power, an influence on
Imagism. But Symbolism held that a poem need not obviously
relate to realities outside itself, that it was its own verbal world.

Thomas's early Notebook poetry often illustrated similar as-
sumptions, but his first successful poems in his own voice were
neither Imagist nor Symbolist in any full sense. He deplored the
emotional poverty and formal thinness of Imagist poems, com-
plaining with characteristic wit that if their nakedly presented
images were meant to conceal a kernel of meaning, the kernel
appeared too often to be 'on half-pay'. And in contrast to strict
Symbolist aims – whereby poetry aspires to the non-referential
condition of music – it is quite clear that in Thomas's poems the
realities of birth, sex, and death are referentially and very con-
cretely there. The influence deriving from French *symboliste* poets
never amounted to much more in Thomas than his adoption of
certain devices such as the 'systematic derangement of the senses'
in Rimbaud's sonnet 'Voyelles', in the form of the syaesthesia of
poems like 'Especially when the October wind', 'Once it was the
colour of saying' and 'When all my five and country senses':

> When all my five and country senses see,
> The fingers will forget green thumbs and mark
> How, through the halfmoon's vegetable eye,
> Husk of young stars and handful zodiac,
> Love in the frost is pared and wintered by.

Nevertheless, in a *Swansea Grammar School Magazine* essay on
'Modern Poetry' in 1929, when he was sixteen, Thomas had
shown himself to be precociously aware of the wide range of
aspirations that had gone to the making of poetic Modernism.
The revolution and experimentalism of Pound and Eliot's gener-
ation were already literary history by the time he was writing his
first mature poems in the early 1930s. But the way in which that
generation had, under the influence of both *symboliste* and
imagiste writing, freed poetry from ordinary discourse (the need

to 'talk *about*' things in poems) was still a potent, if diffused, legacy. And it was within that general sense of a new freedom that Thomas first found his own voice. With these considerations in mind, he could have said, with Yeats, 'I have no speech but symbol, the pagan speech I made/ Amid the dreams of youth'.

VI

The way in which Thomas's generation coolly absorbed influences that decades earlier had gone into the making of Modernist poetry is seen in the case of two other influences. One was from the revival of interest in the Metaphysical poets of the seventeenth-century, prompted by H.J.C. Grierson's edition of Donne, that made such an impact on Yeats in 1912, and Grierson's edition of *Metaphysical Lyrics and Poems of the Seventeenth Century*, given a seminal review by Eliot in 1921. 'I see the boys of summer' may not furnish the best examples of what Thomas clearly owes to Donne, but it does illustrate the Metaphysical obsession with foreshortening the distance between life and death, constantly imaging each in terms of the other. Indeed, one of the most common effects in Thomas's early verse is what one might term the 'metaphysical shudder', when images of death are given a particular *frisson* because of their juxtaposition with incongruous images of life, as when Donne speaks of 'a bracelet of bright hair about the bone' or Herbert claims that a baby's 'clouts are little winding sheets', or Thomas that 'Here love's damp muscle dries and dies,/ Here break a kiss in no love's quarry'. The wit with which 'dries' enacts its very meaning by withering into 'dies' is itself a sign of life. But that notion of a kiss in the quarry of no love (the grave) is part of a larger visionary wit that in Metaphysical poetry talks of sundials in graves or concedes that 'the grave's a fine and private place,/ But none I think do there embrace'. The early poems have been described (even by Thomas himself) as having the morbidity of Beddoes, but their perspective is enliveningly dual in this way. William Empson drew on his knowledge of Thomas as a person as well as a poet when he said 'You must realise that he was a very witty man, with a very keen though not at all poisoned recognition that the world contains horror as well as delight; his chief power as a stylist is to convey a sickened loathing which somehow at once (within the phrase) enforces a welcome for the eternal necessities of the world'. This ability to make us see, 'within the phrase', that 'the poles are kissing as they cross' owed a good deal to the Metaphysical conceit.

Another influence on modern poetry happened as if by accident. The poems of the Victorian Gerard Manley Hopkins were first published only in 1918. Eliot's generation was by then already in full swing, so that it was natural for Hopkins's influence to fall mainly on the younger poets growing up in the 1920s, whose real decade was to be the 1930s. Thomas's later poems are poems of Hopkinsian 'praise', and reflect the legacy fairly obviously. There is the debt, for example, of the 'hawk on fire' of 'Over Sir John's hill' (1949) to Hopkins's 'The Windhover'. But there were different degrees to which the poets of Thomas's generation absorbed the influence. There was even unashamed imitation. Early Auden, with his delight in trying out other poets' voices, could write good Hopkinsian pastiche, and know it ('Defeats on them like lavas/ Have fallen, fell, kept falling, fell/ On them, poor lovies . . .'). And lesser poets, less wryly, wrote as if they had newly formed Hopkins's verbal excitement themselves.

But elsewhere there was a deeper Hopkinsian influence – not flashy excitement but simply a renewed respect for a feeling of *weight* and *density* in the lines. Noone would immediately think of William Empson's poetry as being Hopkinsian, but poems such as 'Camping Out' clearly recreate Hopkins's relish for moving through language as through a resistant medium:

> And now she cleans her teeth into the lake:
> Gives it (God's grace) for her own bounty's sake
> What morning's pale and the crisp mist debars:
> Its glass of the divine (that Will could break)
> Restores, beyond Nature: or lets Heaven take
> (Itself being dimmed) her pattern, who half awake
> Milks between rocks a straddled sky of stars.

It was this textural density that Thomas pointedly reproduced in his 'Request to Leda (Homage to William Empson)' in 1942:

> Not your winged lust but his must now change suit
> The harp-waked Casanova rakes no change
> The worm is (pinpoint) rational in the fruit.

It is a sign of the authenticity of Thomas's early poems that they absorbed Hopkins's richness without its most obvious effects. An unpublished letter of 1938 shows Thomas tentatively but revealingly pondering the debt:

> I have never read Hopkins with any thoroughness or any real affection. This isn't to say that my poems may not have been influenced by his – I read them first when my 'work' was fluid enough, (perhaps I mean watery enough) to find room for any number of foreign bodies, some of which still unfortunately remain, occupying too much space – but the influence is, I imagine, superficial. This may contradict Treece in his essay [in Treece's *Dylan Thomas*], but it is what I *believe* to be true, (I'm allowing for self-hypnotism) . . . I don't know whether I was ever 'determined' – a slightly self-conscious word, especially if applied to the early, formative period of one's writing when the main thing was not just to produce another poem but, in Laura Riding's phrase, to make one poem less – to make 'a richer texture' than so much English poetry (though I had, then, no literary nationalism), but I think that I was always attracted to the idea of extremely concentrated poetry; I never could like the poetry that allowed itself great breathing spaces, tediums and flatnesses, between *essential* passages; I want, and wanted, every line to be the essence of the poem, even the flourishes, the exaggerations. This, naturally, I never could achieve, but it still remains an ideal for me . . . Later, I realized that this *essential* writing, this writing without concessions – I say 'without concessions' for I think that the only person allowed, in a poem, to take a moment off is the reader – could avoid dullness only if it was dramatically effective at the same time.*

Terms of concentration, of mass and essence ('*essential* passages', '*essential* writing'), evoke the sense in Hopkins that the lines have been sensuously relished and articulated in the mouth, and the whole movement of the verse listened to. They are features that 'I see the boys of summer', without being merely 'Hopkinsian', illustrates throughout. For Thomas as for Hopkins, language is not a cool set of signs pointing to the weight and density of things. Words are themselves 'things', with their own rhythmic, physical, almost autonomous life. Thomas's own most often repeated rule was the need to work 'out from words', not 'towards them'. This emphasises precisely what we meant by saying that ideas are not simply 'carried' by his language. Tropes such as 'Lay the gold tithings barren' or 'The signal moon is zero in their voids' are not thoughts translated because their verbal tangibility is not a

---

* This letter is quoted by kind permission of its recipient, Mr Bob Rees of Swansea, a former schoolfriend of the poet's.

presence to be put by. As already suggested, Ted Hughes was one of the inheritors who best absorbed this kind of example. But if we take an image common to both Hughes's 'Thrushes' –

> the shark's mouth
> That hungers down the blood-smell even to a leak of its own
> Side and devouring of itself –

and Thomas's 'Poem on his Birthday' –

> The rippled seals streak down
> To kill and their own tide daubing blood
> Slides good in the sleek mouth –

we can isolate an essential difference. Hughes still intellectualises the physicality of his verse. Even within its muscled texture, there is a decorous fastidiousness to the syntax ('even to a leak of . . . ', 'and devouring of itself'). It reminds us that the influence of Hopkins and Thomas reached Hughes across a gap tenanted by the Movement.

VII

Other thoughts prompted by 'I see the boys of summer' could, of course, detain us longer. One notices, for example, how strenuous is Thomas's sense of stanzaic form. More than just the consistency of stanzaic *shape*, there is the strict count of 11–7–10–8–8–10 syllables per stanza, broken in only one line; the use of feminine endings, approximately rhymed, in only the first two lines of each stanza; the decision to have only words ending in 's' at the end of lines 3–6 of the first five stanzas. This patterning has affinities, whether conscious or not, with the central characteristic of the Welsh-language poetic tradition – its delight in difficult, resistant form. It is a characteristic that in early 'Anglo-Welsh' verse would have been instinctive (in the Welsh-speaking Henry Vaughan in the seventeenth-century, for example). But it had later to be more consciously emulated. Gerard Manley Hopkins actually learned Welsh and imitated a wide range of the effects in that rich tradition. Of the modern Anglo-Welsh poets, Dylan Thomas is far and away the most conscientious user of pre-conceived diffi-cult forms. 'I, in my intricate image' (1935), for example, rhymes on seventy-two words ending in 'l' or 'ls'. And the same delight in hard craft remained unabated in the concertina-ing rhyme scheme of the 102-line 'Prologue' (1952), his last completed poem. ('Why I acrosticked myself like this, don't ask me.') It is no wonder therefore that, for probably the most painful subject he ever attempted – that of his father's approaching blindness and death in 'Do not go gentle into that good night' (finished March 1951) – he used, brilliantly, the daunting form of the villanelle. Few poems in the language better illustrate the truth of Donne's dictum that 'Grief brought to numbers cannot be so fierce,/ For he tames it that fetters it in verse'.

Though his Welsh-speaking parents consciously denied him that language, and despite his disclaimer in the letter above about 'literary nationalism', Thomas would have been aware, through Welsh-speaking friends and his own general interest, of this emphasis on intricacy in the poetic tradition he had been otherwise forced to by-pass. He could say of as early a poem as 'I dreamed my genesis' (1934) that it was 'more or less based on Welsh rhythms, and may seem, rhythmically, a bit strange at first'. That 'more or less' says it all. Like the textural influence of Hopkins, the structural influence of Welsh metrics would have worked through general affinity and analogy rather than close-up imitation, all the more interesting because Hopkins was a channel for the Welsh influence, too. It is not just the geography of Britain, but also its multi-national *variety*, that is ignored when a critic like Alvarez claims that 'England is an island; it is, literally, insulated from the rest of the world'. Though other poems might furnish more extreme examples of this intricate, hidden craft, our sense of the poem as a 'made object' is just as strong in 'I see the boys of summer'. Like all Thomas's work, it avoids a casual voice at every turn, and clarifies the real force of the young Thomas's rejoinder to Stephen Spender – that Spender's poetry 'is so much like poetry, *& so remote from poems*'. This highly-worked quality remained undiminished, despite the simpler narratives of Thomas's later verse. The change from the earlier to the later poetry (the very subject of 'Once it was the colour of saying', 1938) was a case of turning to more ordinary landscapes and a more objective descriptiveness, but in the upshot the stanza-forms and internal echoic patterns of the later poems became even more complicated than those of the earlier ones.

But it is not as constructions or sets of influences that we experience the poems. Their power comes from a unique and resonant voice, one that remains equally characterful in the later, more open, poetry of place:

> The dust of their kettles and clocks swings to and fro
> Where the hay rides now or the bracken kitchens rust
> As the arc of the billhooks that flashed the hedges low
> And cut the birds' boughs that the minstrel sap ran red.
> They from houses where the harvest kneels, hold me hard,
> Who heard the tall bell sail down the Sundays of the dead
> And the rain wring out its tongues on the faded yard.

But whether in that broader, wheeling movement or in the resonance of a single line –

> Love in the frost is pared and wintered by –

it will be clear in this selection that Dylan Thomas sought always to give his poems the force of memorability. And that much never can be obsolete.

WALFORD DAVIES

BRIEF CHRONOLOGY

27 Oct 1914	Dylan Marlais Thomas born in Swansea
Sept 1925	Enters Swansea Grammar School, where his father was Senior English Master
27 Apr 1930	Starts the first of the 'Notebooks' into which he copied his early poems. (The Notebooks continued until Apr 1934)
Aug 1931	Leaves school. Employed as Reporter on the *South Wales Evening Post* (until Dec 1932)
Mar 1933	First poem published in London ('And death shall have no dominion' in the *New English Weekly*)
Aug 1933	First visit to London
Sept 1933	First poem published in 'Poet's Corner' of the *Sunday Referee* ('That Sanity be Kept'). Correspondence with Pamela Hansford Johnson begins
22 Apr 1934	Wins Book Prize of the 'Poet's Corner' – i.e., the *Sunday Referee*'s sponsorship of his first collection of poems
Feb–Nov 1934	Several visits to London
10 Nov 1934	Moves to live in London
18 Dec 1934	*18 Poems* published
Apr 1936	Meets Caitlin Macnamara
10 Sept 1936	*Twenty-five Poems* published
21 Apr 1937	First radio broadcast ('Life and the Modern Poet')
11 Jul 1937	Marries Caitlin Macnamara
May 1938	First moved to live in Laugharne, Carmarthenshire

30 Jan 1939	First son (Llewelyn) born, in Hampshire
24 Aug 1939	*The Map of Love* (poems and stories) published
20 Dec 1939	*The World I Breathe* (a selection of his poetry and prose) – his first volume publication in America
4 Apr 1940	*Portrait of the Artist as a Young Dog* (short stories) published
July 1940	Leaves Laugharne for London
Sept 1940	Begins work as script-writer for films with the Strand Film Company
1940–2	Living partly in London, partly in Wales
Late 1942	Brings wife and son to live in Chelsea
Feb 1943	*New Poems* (USA)
3 Mar 1943	Daughter (Aeronwy) born
1943	Continuous work as broadcaster begins
Sept 1944 –summer 1945	Living at New Quay, Cardiganshire
Summer 1945 –spring 1946	Living in London
7 Feb 1946	*Deaths and Entrances* published
Mar 1946 –May 1949	Living in or near Oxford
8 Nov 1946	*Selected Writings* (USA)
Apr–Aug 1947	Visits Italy
Sept 1947	Moves to live in South Leigh, Oxfordshire
1948	Writing feature films for Gainsborough
Mar 1949	Visits Prague as guest of Czechoslovak government
May 1949	Laugharne again becomes his main home (The Boat House)
24 Jul 1949	Second son (Colm) born

Feb–Jun 1950	First American tour
Jan 1951	In Iran, writing film script for the Anglo Iranian Oil Company
Jan–May 1952	Second American tour
Feb 1952	*In Country Sleep* (USA)
10 Nov 1952	*Collected Poems 1934–1952* published
16 Dec 1952	The poet's father dies
31 Mar 1953	*Collected Poems* (USA)
Apr–Jun 1953	Third American tour
14 May 1953	First performance of *Under Milk Wood* in New York
14 May 1953	*The Doctor and the Devils*. The first of the film scripts to be published
Oct 1953	Leaves on final American tour
9 Nov 1953	Dies in St Vincent's Hospital, New York City

NOTE ON CHRONOLOGY AND TEXT

The poems are arranged chronologically, except for 'Prologue'. If the version in the poet's Notebooks (*The Notebook Poems* 1930–1934, edited by Ralph Maud, Dent 1989) is substantially the same as the one ultimately published (even if of different length), its date becomes that in the Notebook. If the Notebook version was revised to the point where it became substantially a different poem, a later date follows the Notebook date – and if the poem's debt to the Notebook version is minimal, the later date is the only date given. It would be over-fussy to give full bibliographical details, but the dating can be taken to mark the first emergence of a poem's theme and language in ways substantially related to their final character, even if not always their absolutely final form. This is the only way, in a chronological arrangement, to link the essential impulse of a poem to the chronology of the poet's actual life rather than to that of his publishing career. But the reader should remember that the final wording of a poem often came several years after its position in the chronology of this selection. In the case of 'The hunchback in the park' I have made an exception: because of the particularly long gap between that poem's 1941 revision and its 1932 source, I have placed it at the later date. Though fairly fully outlined in its first version, it is stylistically more characteristic of the later phase, and has the extra status of being the very last poem mined from the early Notebooks before their sale to America. Beyond the period of the Notebooks, when dates of composition are circumstantial, they are dates validated either in Thomas's letters or by the fact of first publication.

The text of the 'Collected' poems in this selection is that of *Dylan Thomas: Collected Poems 1934–1953*, edited by Walford Davies and Ralph Maud, Dent, 1988.

1
Prologue

This day winding down now
At God speeded summer's end
In the torrent salmon sun,
In my seashaken house
On a breakneck of rocks   5
Tangled with chirrup and fruit,
Froth, flute, fin and quill
At a wood's dancing hoof,
By scummed, starfish sands
With their fishwife cross   10
Gulls, pipers, cockles, and sails,
Out there, crow black, men
Tackled with clouds, who kneel
To the sunset nets,
Geese nearly in heaven, boys   15
Stabbing, and herons, and shells
That speak seven seas,
Eternal waters away
From the cities of nine
Days' night whose towers will catch   20
In the religious wind
Like stalks of tall, dry straw,
At poor peace I sing
To you, strangers, (though song
Is a burning and crested act,   25
The fire of birds in
The world's turning wood,
For my sawn, splay sounds),
Out of these seathumbed leaves
That will fly and fall   30
Like leaves of trees and as soon
Crumble and undie
Into the dogdayed night.
Seaward the salmon, sucked sun slips,
And the dumb swans drub blue   35

My dabbed bay's dusk, as I hack
This rumpus of shapes
For you to know
How I, a spinning man,
Glory also this star, bird   40
Roared, sea born, man torn, blood blest.
Hark: I trumpet the place,
From fish to jumping hill! Look:
I build my bellowing ark
To the best of my love   45
As the flood begins,
Out of the fountainhead
Of fear, rage red, manalive,
Molten and mountainous to stream
Over the wound asleep   50
Sheep white hollow farms

To Wales in my arms.
Hoo, there, in castle keep,
You king singsong owls, who moonbeam
The flickering runs and dive   55
The dingle furred deer dead!
Huloo, on plumbed bryns,
O my ruffled ring dove
In the hooting, nearly dark
With Welsh and reverent rook,   60
Coo rooing the woods' praise,
Who moons her blue notes from her nest
Down to the curlew herd!
Ho, hullaballoing clan
Agape, with woe   65
In your beaks, on the gabbing capes!
Heigh, on horseback hill, jack
Whisking hare! who
Hears, there, this fox light, my flood ship's
Clangour as I hew and smite   70
(A clash of anvils for my
Hubbub and fiddle, this tune
On a tongued puffball)
But animals thick as thieves
On God's rough tumbling grounds   75

(Hail to His beasthood!).
Beasts who sleep good and thin,
Hist, in hogsback woods! The haystacked
Hollow farms in a throng
Of waters cluck and cling,   80
And barnroofs cockcrow war!
O kingdom of neighbours, finned
Felled and quilled, flash to my patch
Work ark and the moonshine
Drinking Noah of the bay,   85
With pelt, and scale, and fleece:
Only the drowned deep bells
Of sheep and churches noise
Poor peace as the sun sets
And dark shoals every holy field.   90
We shall ride out alone, and then,
Under the stars of Wales,
Cry, Multitudes of arks! Across
The water lidded lands,
Manned with their loves they'll move,   95
Like wooden islands, hill to hill.
Huloo, my prowed dove with a flute!
Ahoy, old, sea-legged fox,
Tom tit and Dai mouse!
My ark sings in the sun   100
At God speeded summer's end
And the flood flowers now.

2

The spire cranes

The spire cranes. Its statue is an aviary.
From the stone nest it does not let the feathery
Carved birds blunt their striking throats on the salt gravel,
Pierce the spilt sky with diving wing in weed and heel
An inch in froth. Chimes cheat the prison spire, pelter   5

In time like outlaw rains on that priest, water,
Time for the swimmers' hands, music for silver lock
And mouth. Both note and plume plunge from the spire's hook.
Those craning birds are choice for you, songs that jump back
To the built voice, or fly with winter to the bells,   10
But do not travel down dumb wind like prodigals.

3
Being but men

Being but men, we walked into the trees
Afraid, letting our syllables be soft
For fear of waking the rooks,
For fear of coming
Noiselessly into a world of wings and cries.   5

If we were children we might climb,
Catch the rooks sleeping, and break no twig,
And, after the soft ascent,
Thrust out our heads above the branches
To wonder at the unfailing stars.   10

Out of confusion, as the way is,
And the wonder that man knows,
Out of the chaos would come bliss.

That, then, is loveliness, we said,
Children in wonder watching the stars,   15
Is the aim and the end.

Being but men, we walked into the trees.

4
Out of the sighs

Out of the sighs a little comes,
But not of grief, for I have knocked down that
Before the agony; the spirit grows,
Forgets, and cries;
A little comes, is tasted and found good;   5
All could not disappoint;
There must, be praised, some certainty,
If not of loving well, then not,
And that is true after perpetual defeat.

After such fighting as the weakest know,   10
There's more than dying;
Lose the great pains or stuff the wound,
He'll ache too long
Through no regret of leaving woman waiting
For her soldier stained with spilt words   15
That spill such acrid blood.

Were that enough, enough to ease the pain,
Feeling regret when this is wasted
That made me happy in the sun,
And, sleeping, made me dream   20
How much was happy while it lasted,
Were vaguenesses enough and the sweet lies plenty,
The hollow words could bear all suffering
And cure me of ills.

Were that enough, bone, blood, and sinew,   25
The twisted brain, the fair-formed loin,
Groping for matter under the dog's plate,
Man should be cured of distemper.
For all there is to give I offer:
Crumbs, barn, and halter.   30

5
Out of a war of wits

Out of a war of wits, when folly of words
Was the world's to me, and syllables
Fell hard as whips on an old wound,
My brain came crying into the fresh light,
Called for confessor but there was none　　　　　5
To purge after the wits' fight,
And I was struck dumb by the sun.
Praise that my body be whole, I've limbs,
Not stumps, after the hour of battle,
For the body's brittle and the skin's white.　　　　10
Praise that only the wits are hurt after the wits' fight.
Overwhelmed by the sun, with a torn brain
I stand beneath the clouds' confessional,
But the hot beams rob me of speech,
After the perils of friends' talk　　　　　15
Reach asking arms up to the milky sky,
After a volley of questions and replies
Lift wit-hurt head for sun to sympathize,
And the sun heals, closing sore eyes.
It is good that the sun shine,　　　　　20
And, after it has sunk, the sane moon,
For out of a house of matchboard and stone
Where men would argue till the stars be green,
It is good to step onto the earth, alone,
And be struck dumb, if only for a time.　　　　25

6
Their faces shone under some radiance

Their faces shone under some radiance
Of mingled moonlight and lamplight
That turned the empty kisses into meaning,
The island of such penny love
Into a costly country, the graves   5
That neighboured them to wells of warmth,
(And skeletons had sap). One minute
Their faces shone; the midnight rain
Hung pointed in the wind,
Before the moon shifted and the sap ran out,   10
She, in her cheap frock, saying some cheap thing,
And he replying,
Not knowing radiance came and passed.
The suicides parade again, now ripe for dying.

7
I have longed to move away

I have longed to move away
From the hissing of the spent lie
And the old terrors' continual cry
Growing more terrible as the day
Goes over the hill into the deep sea;   5
I have longed to move away
From the repetition of salutes,
For there are ghosts in the air
And ghostly echoes on paper,
And the thunder of calls and notes.   10

I have longed to move away but am afraid;
Some life, yet unspent, might explode
Out of the old lie burning on the ground,
And, crackling into the air, leave me half-blind.
Neither by night's ancient fear,   15
The parting of hat from hair,
Pursed lips at the receiver,
Shall I fall to death's feather.
By these I would not care to die,
Half convention and half lie.   20

8
And death shall have no dominion

And death shall have no dominion.
Dead men naked they shall be one
With the man in the wind and the west moon;
When their bones are picked clean and the clean bones gone,
They shall have stars at elbow and foot;   5
Though they go mad they shall be sane,
Though they sink through the sea they shall rise again;
Though lovers be lost love shall not;
And death shall have no dominion.

And death shall have no dominion.   10
Under the windings of the sea
They lying long shall not die windily;
Twisting on racks when sinews give way,
Strapped to a wheel, yet they shall not break;
Faith in their hands shall snap in two,   15
And the unicorn evils run them through;
Split all ends up they shan't crack;
And death shall have no dominion.

And death shall have no dominion.
No more may gulls cry at their ears   20

Or waves break loud on the seashores;
Where blew a flower may a flower no more
Lift its head to the blows of the rain;
Though they be mad and dead as nails,
Heads of the characters hammer through daisies;   25
Break in the sun till the sun breaks down,
And death shall have no dominion.

9
We lying by seasand

We lying by seasand, watching yellow
And the grave sea, mock who deride
Who follow the red rivers, hollow
Alcove of words out of cicada shade,
For in this yellow grave of sand and sea   5
A calling for colour calls with the wind
That's grave and gay as grave and sea
Sleeping on either hand.
The lunar silences, the silent tide
Lapping the still canals, the dry tide-master   10
Ribbed between desert and water storm,
Should cure our ills of the water
With a one-coloured calm;
The heavenly music over the sand
Sounds with the grains as they hurry   15
Hiding the golden mountains and mansions
Of the grave, gay, seaside land.
Bound by a sovereign strip, we lie,
Watch yellow, wish for wind to blow away
The strata of the shore and drown red rock;   20
But wishes breed not, neither
Can we fend off rock arrival,
Lie watching yellow until the golden weather
Breaks, O my heart's blood, like a heart and hill.

10
Ears in the turrets hear

Ears in the turrets hear
Hands grumble on the door,
Eyes in the gables see
The fingers at the locks.
Shall I unbolt or stay   5
Alone till the day I die
Unseen by stranger-eyes
In this white house?
Hands, hold you poison or grapes?

Beyond this island bound   10
By a thin sea of flesh
And a bone coast,
The land lies out of sound
And the hills out of mind.
No bird or flying fish   15
Disturbs this island's rest.

Ears in this island hear
The wind pass like a fire,
Eyes in this island see
Ships anchor off the bay.   20
Shall I run to the ships
With the wind in my hair,
Or stay till the day I die
And welcome no sailor?
Ships, hold you poison or grapes?   25

Hands grumble on the door,
Ships anchor off the bay,
Rain beats the sand and slates.
Shall I let in the stranger,
Shall I welcome the sailor,   30
Or stay till the day I die?

Hands of the stranger and holds of the ships,
Hold you poison or grapes?

11
Here in this spring

Here in this spring, stars float along the void;
Here in this ornamental winter
Down pelts the naked weather;
This summer buries a spring bird.

Symbols are selected from the years'   5
Slow rounding of four seasons' coasts,
In autumn teach three seasons' fires
And four birds' notes.

I should tell summer from the trees, the worms
Tell, if at all, the winter's storms   10
Or the funeral of the sun;
I should learn spring by the cuckooing,
And the slug should teach me destruction.

A worm tells summer better than the clock,
The slug's a living calendar of days;   15
What shall it tell me if a timeless insect
Says the world wears away?

12
Why east wind chills

Why east wind chills and south wind cools
Shall not be known till windwell dries
And west's no longer drowned
In winds that bring the fruit and rind
Of many a hundred falls;   5

Why silk is soft and the stone wounds
The child shall question all his days,
Why night-time rain and the breast's blood
Both quench his thirst he'll have a black reply.

When cometh Jack Frost? the children ask.   10
Shall they clasp a comet in their fists?
Not till, from high and low, their dust
Sprinkles in children's eyes a long-last sleep
And dusk is crowded with the children's ghosts,
Shall a white answer echo from the rooftops.   15

All things are known: the stars' advice
Calls some content to travel with the winds,
Though what the stars ask as they round
Time upon time the towers of the skies
Is heard but little till the stars go out.   20
I hear content, and 'Be content'
Ring like a handbell through the corridors,
And 'Know no answer,' and I know
No answer to the children's cry
Of echo's answer and the man of frost   25
And ghostly comets over the raised fists.

13
The hand that signed the paper

The hand that signed the paper felled a city;
Five sovereign fingers taxed the breath,
Doubled the globe of dead and halved a country;
These five kings did a king to death.

The mighty hand leads to a sloping shoulder,   5
The finger joints are cramped with chalk;
A goose's quill has put an end to murder
That put an end to talk.

The hand that signed the treaty bred a fever,
And famine grew, and locusts came;   10

Great is the hand that holds dominion over
Man by a scribbled name.

The five kings count the dead but do not soften
The crusted wound nor stroke the brow;
A hand rules pity as a hand rules heaven;   15
Hands have no tears to flow.

14
That sanity be kept

That sanity be kept I sit at open windows,
Regard the sky, make unobtrusive comment on the moon,
Sit at open windows in my shirt,
And let the traffic pass, the signals shine,
The engines run, the brass bands keep in tune,   5
For sanity must be preserved.

Thinking of death, I sit and watch the park
Where children play in all their innocence,
And matrons on the littered grass
Absorb the daily sun.   10

The sweet suburban music from a hundred lawns
Comes softly to my ears. The English mowers mow and mow.

I mark the couples walking arm in arm,
Observe their smiles,
Sweet invitations and inventions,   15
See them lend love illustration
By gesture and grimace.
I watch them curiously, detect beneath the laughs
What stands for grief, a vague bewilderment
At things not turning right.   20

I sit at open windows in my shirt,
Observe, like some Jehovah of the west
What passes by, that sanity be kept.

15
Before I knocked

Before I knocked and flesh let enter,
With liquid hands tapped on the womb,
I who was shapeless as the water
That shaped the Jordan near my home
Was brother to Mnetha's daughter   5
And sister to the fathering worm.

I who was deaf to spring and summer,
Who knew not sun nor moon by name,
Felt thud beneath my flesh's armour,
As yet was in a molten form,   10
The leaden stars, the rainy hammer
Swung by my father from his dome.

I knew the message of the winter,
The darted hail, the childish snow,
And the wind was my sister suitor;   15
Wind in me leaped, the hellborn dew;
My veins flowed with the Eastern weather;
Ungotten I knew night and day.

As yet ungotten, I did suffer;
The rack of dreams my lily bones   20
Did twist into a living cipher,
And flesh was snipped to cross the lines
Of gallow crosses on the liver
And brambles in the wringing brains.

My throat knew thirst before the structure   25
Of skin and vein around the well
Where words and water make a mixture
Unfailing till the blood runs foul;
My heart knew love, my belly hunger;
I smelt the maggot in my stool.   30

And time cast forth my mortal creature
To drift or drown upon the seas
Acquainted with the salt adventure
Of tides that never touch the shores.
I who was rich was made the richer   35
By sipping at the vine of days.

I, born of flesh and ghost, was neither
A ghost nor man, but mortal ghost.
And I was struck down by death's feather.
I was mortal to the last   40
Long breath that carried to my father
The message of his dying christ.

You who bow down at cross and altar,
Remember me and pity Him
Who took my flesh and bone for armour   45
And doublecrossed my mother's womb.

16
My hero bares his nerves

My hero bares his nerves along my wrist
That rules from wrist to shoulder,
Unpacks the head that, like a sleepy ghost,
Leans on my mortal ruler,
The proud spine spurning turn and twist.   5

And these poor nerves so wired to the skull
Ache on the lovelorn paper
I hug to love with my unruly scrawl
That utters all love hunger
And tells the page the empty ill.   10

My hero bares my side and sees his heart
Tread, like a naked Venus,
The beach of flesh, and wind her bloodred plait;
Stripping my loin of promise,
He promises a secret heat.   15

He holds the wire from this box of nerves
Praising the mortal error
Of birth and death, the two sad knaves of thieves,
And the hunger's emperor;
He pulls the chain, the cistern moves.   20

17
Song

Love me, not as the dreaming nurses
My falling lungs, nor as the cypress
In his age the lass's clay.
Love me and lift your mask.

Love me, not as the girls of heaven   5
Their airy lovers, nor the mermaiden
Her salty lovers in the sea.
Love me and lift your mask.

Love me, not as the ruffling pigeon
The tops of trees, nor as the legion   10
Of the gulls the lip of waves.
Love me and lift your mask.

Love me, as loves the mole his darkness
And the timid deer the tigress:
Hate and fear be your two loves.   15
Love me and lift your mask.

18
The force that through the green fuse

The force that through the green fuse drives the flower
Drives my green age; that blasts the roots of trees
Is my destroyer.
And I am dumb to tell the crooked rose
My youth is bent by the same wintry fever.   5

The force that drives the water through the rocks
Drives my red blood; that dries the mouthing streams
Turns mine to wax.
And I am dumb to mouth unto my veins
How at the mountain spring the same mouth sucks.   10

The hand that whirls the water in the pool
Stirs the quicksand; that ropes the blowing wind
Hauls my shroud sail.
And I am dumb to tell the hanging man
How of my clay is made the hangman's lime.   15

The lips of time leech to the fountain head;
Love drips and gathers, but the fallen blood
Shall calm her sores.
And I am dumb to tell a weather's wind
How time has ticked a heaven round the stars.   20

And I am dumb to tell the lover's tomb
How at my sheet goes the same crooked worm.

19
Light breaks where no sun shines

Light breaks where no sun shines;
Where no sea runs, the waters of the heart
Push in their tides;
And, broken ghosts with glow-worms in their heads,
The things of light   5
File through the flesh where no flesh decks the bones.

A candle in the thighs
Warms youth and seed and burns the seeds of age;
Where no seed stirs,
The fruit of man unwrinkles in the stars,   10
Bright as a fig;
Where no wax is, the candle shows its hairs.

Dawn breaks behind the eyes;
From poles of skull and toe the windy blood
Slides like a sea;   15
Nor fenced, nor staked, the gushers of the sky
Spout to the rod
Divining in a smile the oil of tears.

Night in the sockets rounds,
Like some pitch moon, the limit of the globes;   20
Day lights the bone;
Where no cold is, the skinning gales unpin
The winter's robes;
The film of spring is hanging from the lids.

Light breaks on secret lots,   25
On tips of thought where thoughts smell in the rain;
When logics die,
The secret of the soil grows through the eye,
And blood jumps in the sun;
Above the waste allotments the dawn halts.   30

20

from A Letter to my Aunt

Discussing the Correct Approach to Modern Poetry

To you, my aunt, who would explore
The literary Chankley Bore,
The paths are hard, for you are not
A literary Hottentot
But just a kind and cultured dame   5
Who knows not Eliot (to her shame).

Fie on you, aunt, that you should see
No genius in David G.,
No elemental form and sound
In T.S.E. and Ezra Pound.   10
Fie on you, aunt! I'll show you how
To elevate your middle brow,
And how to scale and see the sights
From modernist Parnassian heights.

First buy a hat, no Paris model   15
But one the Swiss wear when they yodel,
A bowler thing with one or two
Feathers to conceal the view;
And then in sandals walk the street
(All modern painters use their feet   20
For painting, on their canvas strips,
Their wives or mothers minus hips) . . .

Perhaps it would be best if you
Created something very new,
A dirty novel done in Erse   25
Or written backwards in Welsh verse,
Or paintings on the backs of vests,
Or Sanskrit psalms on lepers' chests.
But if this proved imposs-i-ble
Perhaps it would be just as well,   30
For you could then write what you please,
And modern verse is done with ease.

Do not forget that 'limpet' rhymes
With 'strumpet' in these troubled times,
And commas are the worst of crimes;   35
Few understand the works of Cummings,
And few James Joyce's mental slummings,
And few young Auden's coded chatter;
But then it is the few that matter.
Never be lucid, never state,   40
If you would be regarded great,
The simplest thought or sentiment,
(For thought, we know, is decadent);
Never omit such vital words
As belly, genitals, and —,   45

For these are things that play a part
(And what a part) in all good art.
Remember this: each rose is wormy,
And every lovely woman's germy;
Remember this: that love depends   50
On how the Gallic letter bends;
Remember, too, that life is hell
And even heaven has a smell
Of putrefying angels who
Make deadly whoopee in the blue.   55
These things remembered, what can stop
A poet going to the top?

A final word: before you start
The convulsions of your art,
Remove your brains, take out your heart;   60
Minus these curses, you can be
A genius like David G.

Take courage, aunt, and send your stuff
To Geoffrey Grigson with my luff,
And may I yet live to admire   65
How well your poems light the fire.

21

This bread I break

This bread I break was once the oat,
This wine upon a foreign tree
Plunged in its fruit;
Man in the day or wind at night
Laid the crops low, broke the grape's joy.   5

Once in this wine the summer blood
Knocked in the flesh that decked the vine,
Once in this bread
The oat was merry in the wind;
Man broke the sun, pulled the wind down.   10

This flesh you break, this blood you let
Make desolation in the vein,
Were oat and grape
Born of the sensual root and sap;
My wine you drink, my bread you snap.   15

22
When once the twilight locks

When once the twilight locks no longer
Locked in the long worm of my finger
Nor dammed the sea that sped about my fist,
The mouth of time sucked, like a sponge,
The milky acid on each hinge,   5
And swallowed dry the waters of the breast.

When the galactic sea was sucked
And all the dry seabed unlocked,
I sent my creature scouting on the globe,
That globe itself of hair and bone   10
That, sewn to me by nerve and brain,
Had stringed my flask of matter to his rib.

My fuses timed to charge his heart,
He blew like powder to the light
And held a little sabbath with the sun,   15
But when the stars, assuming shape,
Drew in his eyes the straws of sleep,
He drowned his father's magics in a dream.

All issue armoured, of the grave,
The redhaired cancer still alive,   20
The cataracted eyes that filmed their cloth;
Some dead undid their bushy jaws,
And bags of blood let out their flies;
He had by heart the Christ-cross-row of death.

Sleep navigates the tides of time;   25
The dry Sargasso of the tomb
Gives up its dead to such a working sea;
And sleep rolls mute above the beds
Where fishes' food is fed the shades
Who periscope through flowers to the sky.   30

The hanged who lever from the limes
Ghostly propellers for their limbs,
The cypress lads who wither with the cock,
These, and the others in sleep's acres,
Of dreaming men make moony suckers,   35
And snipe the fools of vision in the back.

When once the twilight screws were turned,
And mother milk was stiff as sand,
I sent my own ambassador to light;
By trick or chance he fell asleep   40
And conjured up a carcase shape
To rob me of my fluids in his heart.

Awake, my sleeper, to the sun,
A worker in the morning town,
And leave the poppied pickthank where he lies;   45
The fences of the light are down,
All but the briskest riders thrown,
And worlds hang on the trees.

23

Where once the waters of your face

Where once the waters of your face
Spun to my screws, your dry ghost blows,
The dead turns up its eye;
Where once the mermen through your ice
Pushed up their hair, the dry wind steers   5

Through salt and root and roe.

Where once your green knots sank their splice
Into the tided cord, there goes
The green unraveller,
His scissors oiled, his knife hung loose   10
To cut the channels at their source
And lay the wet fruits low.

Invisible, your clocking tides
Break on the lovebeds of the weeds;
The weed of love's left dry;   15
There round about your stones the shades
Of children go who, from their voids,
Cry to the dolphined sea.

Dry as a tomb, your coloured lids
Shall not be latched while magic glides   20
Sage on the earth and sky;
There shall be corals in your beds,
There shall be serpents in your tides,
Till all our sea-faiths die.

24
Our eunuch dreams

I

Our eunuch dreams, all seedless in the light,
Of light and love, the tempers of the heart,
Whack their boys' limbs,
And, winding-footed in their shawl and sheet,
Groom the dark brides, the widows of the night   5
Fold in their arms.

The shades of girls, all flavoured from their shrouds,
When sunlight goes are sundered from the worm,
The bones of men, the broken in their beds,
By midnight pulleys that unhouse the tomb.   10

II

In this our age the gunman and his moll,
Two one-dimensioned ghosts, love on a reel,
Strange to our solid eye,
And speak their midnight nothings as they swell;
When cameras shut they hurry to their hole   15
Down in the yard of day.

They dance between their arclamps and our skull,
Impose their shots, throwing the nights away;
We watch the show of shadows kiss or kill,
Flavoured of celluloid give love the lie.   20

III

Which is the world? Of our two sleepings, which
Shall fall awake when cures and their itch
Raise up this red-eyed earth?
Pack off the shapes of daylight and their starch,
The sunny gentlemen, the Welshing rich,   25
Or drive the night-geared forth.

The photograph is married to the eye,
Grafts on its bride one-sided skins of truth;
The dream has sucked the sleeper of his faith
That shrouded men might marrow as they fly.   30

IV

This is the world: the lying likeness of
Our strips of stuff that tatter as we move
Loving and being loth;
The dream that kicks the buried from their sack
And lets their trash be honoured as the quick.   35
This is the world. Have faith.

For we shall be a shouter like the cock,
Blowing the old dead back; our shots shall smack
The image from the plates;
And we shall be fit fellows for a life,   40
And who remain shall flower as they love,
Praise to our faring hearts.

25
I see the boys of summer

I

I see the boys of summer in their ruin
Lay the gold tithings barren,
Setting no store by harvest, freeze the soils;
There in their heat the winter floods
Of frozen loves they fetch their girls,   5
And drown the cargoed apples in their tides.

These boys of light are curdlers in their folly,
Sour the boiling honey;
The jacks of frost they finger in the hives;
There in the sun the frigid threads   10
Of doubt and dark they feed their nerves;
The signal moon is zero in their voids.

I see the summer children in their mothers
Split up the brawned womb's weathers,
Divide the night and day with fairy thumbs;   15
There in the deep with quartered shades
Of sun and moon they paint their dams
As sunlight paints the shelling of their heads.

I see that from these boys shall men of nothing
Stature by seedy shifting,   20
Or lame the air with leaping from its heats;
There from their hearts the dogdayed pulse
Of love and light bursts in their throats.
O see the pulse of summer in the ice.

II

But seasons must be challenged or they totter   25
Into a chiming quarter
Where, punctual as death, we ring the stars;
There, in his night, the black-tongued bells
The sleepy man of winter pulls,
Nor blows back moon-and-midnight as she blows.   30

We are the dark deniers, let us summon
Death from a summer woman,
A muscling life from lovers in their cramp,
From the fair dead who flush the sea
The bright-eyed worm on Davy's lamp,   35
And from the planted womb the man of straw.

We summer boys in this four-winded spinning,
Green of the seaweeds' iron,
Hold up the noisy sea and drop her birds,
Pick the world's ball of wave and froth   40
To choke the deserts with her tides,
And comb the county gardens for a wreath.

In spring we cross our foreheads with the holly,
Heigh ho the blood and berry,
And nail the merry squires to the trees;   45
Here love's damp muscle dries and dies,
Here break a kiss in no love's quarry.
O see the poles of promise in the boys.

III

I see you boys of summer in your ruin.
Man in his maggot's barren.   50
And boys are full and foreign in the pouch.
I am the man your father was.
We are the sons of flint and pitch.
O see the poles are kissing as they cross.

26
If I were tickled by the rub of love

If I were tickled by the rub of love,
A rooking girl who stole me for her side,
Broke through her straws, breaking my bandaged string,
If the red tickle as the cattle calve
Still set to scratch a laughter from my lung,   5
I would not fear the apple nor the flood
Nor the bad blood of spring.

Shall it be male or female? say the cells,
And drop the plum like fire from the flesh.
If I were tickled by the hatching hair,   10
The winging bone that sprouted in the heels,
The itch of man upon the baby's thigh,
I would not fear the gallows nor the axe
Nor the crossed sticks of war.

Shall it be male or female? say the fingers   15
That chalk the walls with green girls and their men.
I would not fear the muscling-in of love
If I were tickled by the urchin hungers
Rehearsing heat upon a raw-edged nerve.
I would not fear the devil in the loin   20
Nor the outspoken grave.

If I were tickled by the lovers' rub
That wipes away not crow's-foot nor the lock
Of sick old manhood on the fallen jaws,
Time and the crabs and the sweethearting crib   25
Would leave me cold as butter for the flies,
The sea of scums could drown me as it broke
Dead on the sweethearts' toes.

This world is half the devil's and my own,
Daft with the drug that's smoking in a girl   30

And curling round the bud that forks her eye.
An old man's shank one-marrowed with my bone,
And all the herrings smelling in the sea,
I sit and watch the worm beneath my nail
Wearing the quick away.   35

And that's the rub, the only rub that tickles.
The knobbly ape that swings along his sex
From damp love-darkness and the nurse's twist
Can never raise the midnight of a chuckle,
Nor when he finds a beauty in the breast   40
Of lover, mother, lovers, or his six
Feet in the rubbing dust.

And what's the rub? Death's feather on the nerve?
Your mouth, my love, the thistle in the kiss?
My Jack of Christ born thorny on the tree?   45
The words of death are dryer than his stiff,
My wordy wounds are printed with your hair.
I would be tickled by the rub that is:
Man be my metaphor.

27

Especially when the October wind

Especially when the October wind
With frosty fingers punishes my hair,
Caught by the crabbing sun I walk on fire
And cast a shadow crab upon the land,
By the sea's side, hearing the noise of birds,   5
Hearing the raven cough in winter sticks,
My busy heart who shudders as she talks
Sheds the syllabic blood and drains her words.

Shut, too, in a tower of words, I mark
On the horizon walking like the trees   10

The wordy shapes of women, and the rows
Of the star-gestured children in the park.
Some let me make you of the vowelled beeches,
Some of the oaken voices, from the roots
Of many a thorny shire tell you notes,   15
Some let me make you of the water's speeches.

Behind a pot of ferns the wagging clock
Tells me the hour's word, the neural meaning
Flies on the shafted disc, declaims the morning
And tells the windy weather in the cock.   20
Some let me make you of the meadow's signs;
The signal grass that tells me all I know
Breaks with the wormy winter through the eye.
Some let me tell you of the raven's sins.

Especially when the October wind   25
(Some let me make you of autumnal spells,
The spider-tongued, and the loud hill of Wales)
With fist of turnips punishes the land,
Some let me make you of the heartless words.
The heart is drained that, spelling in the scurry   30
Of chemic blood, warned of the coming fury.
By the sea's side hear the dark-vowelled birds.

28
Should lanterns shine

Should lanterns shine, the holy face,
Caught in an octagon of unaccustomed light,
Would wither up, and any boy of love
Look twice before he fell from grace.
The features in their private dark   5
Are formed of flesh, but let the false day come
And from her lips the faded pigments fall,
The mummy cloths expose an ancient breast.

I have been told to reason by the heart,
But heart, like head, leads helplessly;   10

I have been told to reason by the pulse,
And, when it quickens, alter the actions' pace
Till field and roof lie level and the same
So fast I move defying time, the quiet gentleman
Whose beard wags in Egyptian wind.   15

I have heard many years of telling,
And many years should see some change.

The ball I threw while playing in the park
Has not yet reached the ground.

29

Altarwise by owl-light

SONNET I

Altarwise by owl-light in the halfway-house
The gentleman lay graveward with his furies;
Abaddon in the hang-nail cracked from Adam,
And, from his fork, a dog among the fairies,
The atlas-eater with a jaw for news,   5
Bit out the mandrake with tomorrow's scream.
Then, penny-eyed, that gentleman of wounds,
Old cock from nowheres and the heaven's egg,
With bones unbuttoned to the halfway winds,
Hatched from the windy salvage on one leg,   10
Scraped at my cradle in a walking word
That night of time under the Christward shelter,
I am the long world's gentleman, he said,
And share my bed with Capricorn and Cancer.

30
Altarwise by owl-light

SONNET IV

What is the metre of the dictionary?
The size of genesis? the short spark's gender?
Shade without shape? the shape of Pharaoh's echo?
(My shape of age nagging the wounded whisper).
Which sixth of wind blew out the burning gentry?   5
(Questions are hunchbacks to the poker marrow).
What of a bamboo man among your acres?
Corset the boneyards for a crooked lad?
Button your bodice on a hump of splinters,
My camel's eye will needle through the shroud.   10
Love's a reflection of the mushroom features,
Stills snapped by night in the bread-sided field,
Once close-up smiling in the wall of pictures,
Ark-lamped thrown back upon the cutting flood.

31
Incarnate devil

Incarnate devil in a talking snake,
The central plains of Asia in his garden,
In shaping-time the circle stung awake,
In shapes of sin forked out the bearded apple,
And God walked there who was a fiddling warden   5
And played down pardon from the heavens' hill.

When we were strangers to the guided seas,
A handmade moon half holy in a cloud,
The wisemen tell me that the garden gods
Twined good and evil on an eastern tree;   10

And when the moon rose windily it was
Black as the beast and paler than the cross.

We in our Eden knew the secret guardian
In sacred waters that no frost could harden,
And in the mighty mornings of the earth;   15
Hell in a horn of sulphur and the cloven myth,
All heaven in a midnight of the sun,
A serpent fiddled in the shaping-time.

32
O make me a mask

O make me a mask and a wall to shut from your spies
Of the sharp, enamelled eyes and the spectacled claws
Rape and rebellion in the nurseries of my face,
Gag of a dumbstruck tree to block from bare enemies
The bayonet tongue in this undefended prayerpiece,   5
The present mouth, and the sweetly blown trumpet of lies,
Shaped in old armour and oak the countenance of a dunce
To shield the glistening brain and blunt the examiners,
And a tear-stained widower grief drooped from the lashes
To veil belladonna and let the dry eyes perceive   10
Others betray the lamenting lies of their losses
By the curve of the nude mouth or the laugh up the sleeve.

33
How shall my animal

How shall my animal
Whose wizard shape I trace in the cavernous skull,
Vessel of abscesses and exultation's shell,
Endure burial under the spelling wall,
The invoked, shrouding veil at the cap of the face,   5

Who should be furious,
Drunk as a vineyard snail, flailed like an octopus,
Roaring, crawling, quarrel
With the outside weathers,
The natural circle of the discovered skies   10
Draw down to its weird eyes?

How shall it magnetize,
Towards the studded male in a bent, midnight blaze
That melts the lionhead's heel and horseshoe of the heart,
A brute land in the cool top of the country days   15
To trot with a loud mate the haybeds of a mile,
Love and labour and kill
In quick, sweet, cruel light till the locked ground sprout out,
The black, burst sea rejoice,
The bowels turn turtle,   20
Claw of the crabbed veins squeeze from each red particle
The parched and raging voice?

Fishermen of mermen
Creep and harp on the tide, sinking their charmed, bent pin
With bridebait of gold bread, I with a living skein,   25
Tongue and ear in the thread, angle the temple-bound
Curl-locked and animal cavepools of spells and bone,
Trace out a tentacle,
Nailed with an open eye, in the bowl of wounds and weed
To clasp my fury on ground   30
And clap its great blood down;
Never shall beast be born to atlas the few seas
Or poise the day on a horn.

Sigh long, clay cold, lie shorn,
Cast high, stunned on gilled stone; sly scissors ground
                                                  in frost   35
Clack through the thicket of strength, love hewn in pillars drops
With carved bird, saint, and sun, the wrackspiked maiden
                                                  mouth
Lops, as a bush plumed with flames, the rant of the fierce eye,
Clips short the gesture of breath.
Die in red feathers when the flying heaven's cut,   40

And roll with the knocked earth:
Lie dry, rest robbed, my beast.
You have kicked from a dark den, leaped up the whinnying
                                    light,
And dug your grave in my breast.

34
When all my five and country senses

When all my five and country senses see,
The fingers will forget green thumbs and mark
How, through the halfmoon's vegetable eye,
Husk of young stars and handfull zodiac,
Love in the frost is pared and wintered by,   5
The whispering ears will watch love drummed away
Down breeze and shell to a discordant beach,
And, lashed to syllables, the lynx tongue cry
That her fond wounds are mended bitterly.
My nostrils see her breath burn like a bush.   10

My one and noble heart has witnesses
In all love's countries, that will grope awake;
And when blind sleep drops on the spying senses,
The heart is sensual, though five eyes break.

35
After the funeral
(In memory of Ann Jones)

After the funeral, mule praises, brays,
Windshake of sailshaped ears, muffle-toed tap
Tap happily of one peg in the thick
Grave's foot, blinds down the lids, the teeth in black,
The spittled eyes, the salt ponds in the sleeves,   5

Morning smack of the spade that wakes up sleep,
Shakes a desolate boy who slits his throat
In the dark of the coffin and sheds dry leaves,
That breaks one bone to light with a judgment clout,
After the feast of tear-stuffed time and thistles   10
In a room with a stuffed fox and a stale fern,
I stand, for this memorial's sake, alone
In the snivelling hours with dead, humped Ann
Whose hooded, fountain heart once fell in puddles
Round the parched worlds of Wales and drowned each sun 15
(Though this for her is a monstrous image blindly
Magnified out of praise; her death was a still drop;
She would not have me sinking in the holy
Flood of her heart's fame; she would lie dumb and deep
And need no druid of her broken body).   20
But I, Ann's bard on a raised hearth, call all
The seas to service that her wood-tongued virtue
Babble like a bellbuoy over the hymning heads,
Bow down the walls of the ferned and foxy woods
That her love sing and swing through a brown chapel,   25
Bless her bent spirit with four, crossing birds.
Her flesh was meek as milk, but this skyward statue
With the wild breast and blessed and giant skull
Is carved from her in a room with a wet window
In a fiercely mourning house in a crooked year.   30
I know her scrubbed and sour humble hands
Lie with religion in their cramp, her threadbare
Whisper in a damp word, her wits drilled hollow,
Her fist of a face died clenched on a round pain;
And sculptured Ann is seventy years of stone.   35
These cloud-sopped, marble hands, this monumental
Argument of the hewn voice, gesture and psalm
Storm me forever over her grave until
The stuffed lung of the fox twitch and cry Love
And the strutting fern lay seeds on the black sill.   40

36
The tombstone told

The tombstone told when she died.
Her two surnames stopped me still.
A virgin married at rest.
She married in this pouring place,
That I struck one day by luck,   5
Before I heard in my mother's side
Or saw in the looking-glass shell
The rain through her cold heart speak
And the sun killed in her face.
More the thick stone cannot tell.   10

Before she lay on a stranger's bed
With a hand plunged through her hair,
Or that rainy tongue beat back
Through the devilish years and innocent deaths
To the room of a secret child,   15
Among men later I heard it said
She cried her white-dressed limbs were bare
And her red lips were kissed black,
She wept in her pain and made mouths,
Talked and tore though her eyes smiled.   20

I who saw in a hurried film
Death and this mad heroine
Meet once on a mortal wall
Heard her speak through the chipped beak
Of the stone bird guarding her: 25
I died before bedtime came
But my womb was bellowing
And I felt with my bare fall
A blazing red harsh head tear up
And the dear floods of his hair.   30

37
On no work of words

On no work of words now for three lean months in the bloody
Belly of the rich year and the big purse of my body
I bitterly take to task my poverty and craft:

To take to give is all, return what is hungrily given
Puffing the pounds of manna up through the dew to heaven,   5
The lovely gift of the gab bangs back on a blind shaft.

To lift to leave from the treasures of man is pleasing death
That will rake at last all currencies of the marked breath
And count the taken, forsaken mysteries in a bad dark.

To surrender now is to pay the expensive ogre twice.   10
Ancient woods of my blood, dash down to the nut of the seas
If I take to burn or return this world which is each man's work.

38
Twenty-four years

Twenty-four years remind the tears of my eyes.
(Bury the dead for fear that they walk to the grave in labour.)
In the groin of the natural doorway I crouched like a tailor
Sewing a shroud for a journey
By the light of the meat-eating sun.   5
Dressed to die, the sensual strut begun,
With my red veins full of money,
In the final direction of the elementary town
I advance for as long as forever is.

39
Once it was the colour of saying

Once it was the colour of saying
Soaked my table the uglier side of a hill
With a capsized field where a school sat still
And a black and white patch of girls grew playing:
The gentle seaslides of saying I must undo   5
That all the charmingly drowned arise to cockcrow and kill.
When I whistled with mitching boys through a reservoir park
Where at night we stoned the cold and cuckoo
Lovers in the dirt of their leafy beds,
The shade of their trees was a word of many shades   10
And a lamp of lightning for the poor in the dark;
Now my saying shall be my undoing,
And every stone I wind off like a reel.

40
If my head hurt a hair's foot

'If my head hurt a hair's foot
Pack back the downed bone. If the unpricked ball of my breath
Bump on a spout let the bubbles jump out.
Sooner drop with the worm of the ropes round my throat
Than bully ill love in the clouted scene.   5

All game phrases fit your ring of a cockfight:
I'll comb the snared woods with a glove on a lamp,
Peck, sprint, dance on fountains and duck time
Before I rush in a crouch the ghost with a hammer, air,
Strike light, and bloody a loud room.   10

If my bunched, monkey coming is cruel
Rage me back to the making house. My hand unravel
When you sew the deep door. The bed is a cross place.
Bend, if my journey ache, direction like an arc or make
A limp and riderless shape to leap nine thinning months.'   15

'No. Not for Christ's dazzling bed
Or a nacreous sleep among soft particles and charms
My dear would I change my tears or your iron head.
Thrust, my daughter or son, to escape, there is none, none, none,
Nor when all ponderous heaven's host of waters breaks.   20

Now to awake husked of gestures and my joy like a cave
To the anguish and carrion, to the infant forever unfree,
O my lost love bounced from a good home;
The grain that hurries this way from the rim of the grave
Has a voice and a house, and there and here you must
                                            couch and cry.   25

Rest beyond choice in the dusk-appointed grain,
At the breast stored with seas. No return
Through the waves of the fat streets nor the skeleton's thin
                                                        ways
The grave and my calm body are shut to your coming as stone,
And the endless beginning of prodigies suffers open.'   30

41
To Others than You

Friend by enemy I call you out.

You with a bad coin in your socket,
You my friend there with a winning air
Who palmed the lie on me when you looked
Brassily at my shyest secret,   5

Enticed with twinkling bits of the eye
Till the sweet tooth of my love bit dry,
Rasped at last, and I stumbled and sucked,
Whom now I conjure to stand as thief
In the memory worked by mirrors,   10
With unforgettably smiling act,
Quickness of hand in the velvet glove
And my whole heart under your hammer,
Were once such a creature, so gay and frank
A desireless familiar   15
I never thought to utter or think
While you displaced a truth in the air,

That though I loved them for their faults
As much as for their good,
My friends were enemies on stilts   20
With their heads in a cunning cloud.

42

When I woke

When I woke, the town spoke.
Birds and clocks and cross bells
Dinned aside the coiling crowd,
The reptile profligates in a flame,
Spoilers and pokers of sleep,   5
The next-door sea dispelled
Frogs and satans and woman-luck,
While a man outside with a billhook,
Up to his head in his blood,
Cutting the morning off,   10
The warm-veined double of Time
And his scarving beard from a book,
Slashed down the last snake as though
It were a wand or subtle bough,
Its tongue peeled in the wrap of a leaf.   15

Every morning I make,
God in bed, good and bad,
After a water-face walk,
The death-stagged scatter-breath
Mammoth and sparrowfall   20
Everybody's earth.
Where birds ride like leaves and boats like ducks
I heard, this morning, waking,
Crossly out of the town noises
A voice in the erected air,   25
No prophet-progeny of mine,
Cry my sea town was breaking.
No Time, spoke the clocks, no God, rang the bells,
I drew the white sheet over the islands
And the coins on my eyelids sang like shells.   30

43
Paper and sticks

Paper and sticks and shovel and match
Why won't the news of the old world catch
And the fire in a temper start

Once I had a rich boy for myself
I loved his body and his navy blue wealth   5
And I lived in his purse and his heart

When in our bed I was tossing and turning
All I could see were his brown eyes burning
By the green of a one pound note

I talk to him as I clean the grate   10
O my dear it's never too late
To take me away as you whispered and wrote

I had a handsome and well-off boy
I'll share my money and we'll run for joy
With a bouncing and silver spooned kid   15

Sharp and shrill my silly tongue scratches
Words on the air as the fire catches
You never did and *he* never did.

44

There was a saviour

There was a saviour
    Rarer than radium,
Commoner than water, crueller than truth;
    Children kept from the sun
    Assembled at his tongue   5
To hear the golden note turn in a groove,
Prisoners of wishes locked their eyes
In the jails and studies of his keyless smiles.

    The voice of children says
    From a lost wilderness   10
There was calm to be done in his safe unrest,
    When hindering man hurt
    Man, animal, or bird
We hid our fears in that murdering breath,
Silence, silence to do, when earth grew loud,   15
In lairs and asylums of the tremendous shout.

    There was glory to hear
    In the churches of his tears,
Under his downy arm you sighed as he struck,
    O you who could not cry   20
    On to the ground when a man died
Put a tear for joy in the unearthly flood
And laid your cheek against a cloud-formed shell:
Now in the dark there is only yourself and myself.

Two proud, blacked brothers cry, 25
Winter-locked side by side,
To this inhospitable hollow year,
O we who could not stir
One lean sigh when we heard
Greed on man beating near and fire neighbour 30
But wailed and nested in the sky-blue wall
Now break a giant tear for the little known fall,

For the drooping of homes
That did not nurse our bones,
Brave deaths of only ones but never found, 35
Now see, alone in us,
Our own true strangers' dust
Ride through the doors of our unentered house.
Exiled in us we arouse the soft,
Unclenched, armless, silk and rough love that breaks all rocks. 40

45
Deaths and Entrances

On almost the incendiary eve
Of several near deaths,
When one at the great least of your best loved
And always known must leave
Lions and fires of his flying breath, 5
Of your immortal friends
Who'd raise the organs of the counted dust
To shoot and sing your praise,
One who called deepest down shall hold his peace
That cannot sink or cease 10
Endlessly to his wound
In many married London's estranging grief.

On almost the incendiary eve
When at your lips and keys,
Locking, unlocking, the murdered strangers weave, 15

One who is most unknown,
Your polestar neighbour, sun of another street,
   Will dive up to his tears.
He'll bathe his raining blood in the male sea
   Who strode for your own dead   20
And wind his globe out of your water thread
   And load the throats of shells
   With every cry since light
Flashed first across his thunderclapping eyes.

On almost the incendiary eve   25
   Of deaths and entrances,
When near and strange wounded on London's waves
   Have sought your single grave,
One enemy, of many, who knows well
   Your heart is luminous   30
In the watched dark, quivering through locks and caves,
   Will pull the thunderbolts
To shut the sun, plunge, mount your darkened keys
   And sear just riders back,
   Until that one loved least   35
Looms the last Samson of your zodiac.

46

On the Marriage of a Virgin

Waking alone in a multitude of loves when morning's light
Surprised in the opening of her nightlong eyes
His golden yesterday asleep upon the iris
And this day's sun leapt up the sky out of her thighs
Was miraculous virginity old as loaves and fishes,   5
Though the moment of a miracle is unending lightning
And the shipyards of Galilee's footprints hide a navy of doves.

No longer will the vibrations of the sun desire on
Her deepsea pillow where once she married alone,
Her heart all ears and eyes, lips catching the avalanche   10

Of the golden ghost who ringed with his streams her mercury
                                        bone,
Who under the lids of her windows hoisted his golden luggage,
For a man sleeps where fire leapt down and she learns through
                                        his arm
That other sun, the jealous coursing of the unrivalled blood.

47
Ballad of the Long-legged Bait

The bows glided down, and the coast
Blackened with birds took a last look
At his thrashing hair and whale-blue eye;
The trodden town rang its cobbles for luck.

Then goodbye to the fishermanned   5
Boat with its anchor free and fast
As a bird hooking over the sea,
High and dry by the top of the mast,

Whispered the affectionate sand
And the bulwarks of the dazzled quay.   10
For my sake sail, and never look back,
Said the looking land.

Sails drank the wind, and white as milk
He sped into the drinking dark;
The sun shipwrecked west on a pearl   15
And the moon swam out of its hulk.

Funnels and masts went by in a whirl.
Goodbye to the man on the sea-legged deck
To the gold gut that sings on his reel
To the bait that stalked out of the sack,   20

For we saw him throw to the swift flood
A girl alive with his hooks through her lips;
All the fishes were rayed in blood,
Said the dwindling ships.

Goodbye to chimneys and funnels,   25

Old wives that spin in the smoke,
He was blind to the eyes of candles
In the praying windows of waves

But heard his bait buck in the wake
And tussle in a shoal of loves.   30
Now cast down your rod, for the whole
Of the sea is hilly with whales,

She longs among horses and angels,
The rainbow-fish bend in her joys,
Floated the lost cathedral   35
Chimes of the rocked buoys.

Where the anchor rode like a gull
Miles over the moonstruck boat
A squall of birds bellowed and fell,
A cloud blew the rain from its throat;   40

He saw the storm smoke out to kill
With fuming bows and ram of ice,
Fire on starlight, rake Jesu's stream;
And nothing shone on the water's face

But the oil and bubble of the moon,   45
Plunging and piercing in his course
The lured fish under the foam
Witnessed with a kiss.

Whales in the wake like capes and Alps
Quaked the sick sea and snouted deep,   50
Deep the great bushed bait with raining lips
Slipped the fins of those humpbacked tons

And fled their love in a weaving dip.
Oh, Jericho was falling in their lungs!
She nipped and dived in the nick of love,   55
Spun on a spout like a long-legged ball

Till every beast blared down in a swerve
Till every turtle crushed from his shell
Till every bone in the rushing grave
Rose and crowed and fell!   60

Good luck to the hand on the rod,
There is thunder under its thumbs;
Gold gut is a lightning thread,
His fiery reel sings off its flames,

The whirled boat in the burn of his blood   65
Is crying from nets to knives,
Oh the shearwater birds and their boatsized brood
Oh the bulls of Biscay and their calves

Are making under the green, laid veil
The long-legged beautiful bait their wives.   70
Break the black news and paint on a sail
Huge weddings in the waves,

Over the wakeward-flashing spray
Over the gardens of the floor
Clash out the mounting dolphin's day,   75
My mast is a bell-spire,

Strike and smoothe, for my decks are drums,
Sing through the water-spoken prow
The octopus walking into her limbs
The polar eagle with his tread of snow.   80

From salt-lipped beak to the kick of the stern
Sing how the seal has kissed her dead!
The long, laid minute's bride drifts on
Old in her cruel bed.

Over the graveyard in the water   85
Mountains and galleries beneath
Nightingale and hyena
Rejoicing for that drifting death

Sing and howl through sand and anemone
Valley and sahara in a shell,   90
Oh all the wanting flesh his enemy
Thrown to the sea in the shell of a girl

Is old as water and plain as an eel;
Always goodbye to the long-legged bread
Scattered in the paths of his heels   95

For the salty birds fluttered and fed

And the tall grains foamed in their bills;
Always goodbye to the fires of the face,
For the crab-backed dead on the sea-bed rose
And scuttled over her eyes,   100

The blind, clawed stare is cold as sleet.
The tempter under the eyelid
Who shows to the selves asleep
Mast-high moon-white women naked

Walking in wishes and lovely for shame   105
Is dumb and gone with his flame of brides.
Susanna's drowned in the bearded stream
And no-one stirs at Sheba's side

But the hungry kings of the tides;
Sin who had a woman's shape   110
Sleeps till Silence blows on a cloud
And all the lifted waters walk and leap.

Lucifer that bird's dropping
Out of the sides of the north
Has melted away and is lost   115
Is always lost in her vaulted breath.

Venus lies star-struck in her wound
And the sensual ruins make
Seasons over the liquid world,
White springs in the dark.   120

Always goodbye, cried the voices through the shell,
Goodbye always for the flesh is cast
And the fisherman winds his reel
With no more desire than a ghost.

Always good luck, praised the finned in the feather   125
Bird after dark and the laughing fish
As the sails drank up the hail of thunder
And the long-tailed lightning lit his catch.

The boat swims into the six-year weather,
A wind throws a shadow and it freezes fast.   130

See what the gold gut drags from under
Mountains and galleries to the crest!

See what clings to hair and skull
As the boat skims on with drinking wings!
The statues of great rain stand still,   135
And the flakes fall like hills.

Sing and strike his heavy haul
Toppling up the boatside in a snow of light!
His decks are drenched with miracles.
Oh miracle of fishes! The long dead bite!   140

Out of the urn the size of a man
Out of the room the weight of his trouble
Out of the house that holds a town
In the continent of a fossil

One by one in dust and shawl,   145
Dry as echoes and insect-faced,
His fathers cling to the hand of the girl
And the dead hand leads the past,

Leads them as children and as air
On to the blindly tossing tops;   150
The centuries throw back their hair
And the old men sing from newborn lips:

Time is bearing another son.
Kill Time! She turns in her pain!
The oak is felled in the acorn   155
And the hawk in the egg kills the wren.

He who blew the great fire in
And died on a hiss of flames
Or walked on the earth in the evening
Counting the denials of the grains   160

Clings to her drifting hair, and climbs;
And he who taught their lips to sing
Weeps like the risen sun among
The liquid choirs of his tribes.

The rod bends low, divining land,   165

And through the sundered water crawls
A garden holding to her hand
With birds and animals

With men and women and waterfalls
Trees cool and dry in the whirlpool of ships   170
And stunned and still on the green, laid veil
Sand with legends in its virgin laps

And prophets loud on the burned dunes;
Insects and valleys hold her thighs hard,
Time and places grip her breast bone,   175
She is breaking with seasons and clouds;

Round her trailed wrist fresh water weaves,
With moving fish and rounded stones
Up and down the greater waves
A separate river breathes and runs;   180

Strike and sing his catch of fields
For the surge is sown with barley,
The cattle graze on the covered foam,
The hills have footed the waves away,

With wild sea fillies and soaking bridles   185
With salty colts and gales in their limbs
All the horses of his haul of miracles
Gallop through the arched, green farms,

Trot and gallop with gulls upon them
And thunderbolts in their manes.   190
O Rome and Sodom Tomorrow and London
The country tide is cobbled with towns,

And steeples pierce the cloud on her shoulder
And the streets that the fisherman combed
When his long-legged flesh was a wind on fire   195
And his loin was a hunting flame

Coil from the thoroughfares of her hair
And terribly lead him home alive
Lead her prodigal home to his terror,
The furious ox-killing house of love.   200

Down, down, down, under the ground,
Under the floating villages,
Turns the moon-chained and water-wound
Metropolis of fishes,

There is nothing left of the sea but its sound,   205
Under the earth the loud sea walks,
In deathbeds of orchards the boat dies down
And the bait is drowned among hayricks,

Land, land, land, nothing remains
Of the pacing, famous sea but its speech,   210
And into its talkative seven tombs
The anchor dives through the floors of a church.

Goodbye, good luck, struck the sun and the moon,
To the fisherman lost on the land.
He stands alone at the door of his home,   215
With his long-legged heart in his hand.

48
Love in the Asylum

A stranger has come
To share my room in the house not right in the head,
A girl mad as birds

Bolting the night of the door with her arm her plume.
Strait in the mazed bed   5
She deludes the heaven-proof house with entering clouds

Yet she deludes with walking the nightmarish room,
At large as the dead,
Or rides the imagined oceans of the male wards.

She has come possessed   10
Who admits the delusive light through the bouncing wall,
         Possessed by the skies

She sleeps in the narrow trough yet she walks the dust
         Yet raves at her will
On the madhouse boards worn thin by my walking tears.   15

And taken by light in her arms at long and dear last
         I may without fail
Suffer the first vision that set fire to the stars.

49
The hunchback in the park

The hunchback in the park
A solitary mister
Propped between trees and water
From the opening of the garden lock
That lets the trees and water enter   5
Until the Sunday sombre bell at dark

Eating bread from a newspaper
Drinking water from the chained cup
That the children filled with gravel
In the fountain basin where I sailed my ship   10
Slept at night in a dog kennel
But nobody chained him up.

Like the park birds he came early
Like the water he sat down
And Mister they called Hey mister   15
The truant boys from the town
Running when he had heard them clearly
On out of sound

Past lake and rockery
Laughing when he shook his paper   20

Hunchbacked in mockery
Through the loud zoo of the willow groves
Dodging the park keeper
With his stick that picked up leaves.

And the old dog sleeper   25
Alone between nurses and swans
While the boys among willows
Made the tigers jump out of their eyes
To roar on the rockery stones
And the groves were blue with sailors   30

Made all day until bell time
A woman figure without fault
Straight as a young elm
Straight and tall from his crooked bones
That she might stand in the night   35
After the locks and chains

All night in the unmade park
After the railings and shrubberies
The birds the grass the trees the lake
And the wild boys innocent as strawberries   40
Had followed the hunchback
To his kennel in the dark.

50
Among those Killed in the Dawn Raid
was a Man Aged a Hundred

When the morning was waking over the war
He put on his clothes and stepped out and he died,
The locks yawned loose and a blast blew them wide,
He dropped where he loved on the burst pavement stone
And the funeral grains of the slaughtered floor.   5

Tell his street on its back he stopped a sun
And the craters of his eyes grew springshoots and fire
When all the keys shot from the locks, and rang.
Dig no more for the chains of his grey-haired heart.
The heavenly ambulance drawn by a wound   10
Assembling waits for the spade's ring on the cage.
O keep his bones away from that common cart,
The morning is flying on the wings of his age
And a hundred storks perch on the sun's right hand.

51
Lie still, sleep becalmed

Lie still, sleep becalmed, sufferer with the wound
In the throat, burning and turning. All night afloat
On the silent sea we have heard the sound
That came from the wound wrapped in the salt sheet.

Under the mile off moon we trembled listening   5
To the sea sound flowing like blood from the loud wound
And when the salt sheet broke in a storm of singing
The voices of all the drowned swam on the wind.

Open a pathway through the slow sad sail,
Throw wide to the wind the gates of the wandering boat   10
For my voyage to begin to the end of my wound,
We heard the sea sound sing, we saw the salt sheet tell.
Lie still, sleep becalmed, hide the mouth in the throat,
Or we shall obey, and ride with you through the drowned.

52
Ceremony After a Fire Raid

I

Myselves
The grievers
Grieve
Among the street burned to tireless death
A child of a few hours   5
With its kneading mouth
Charred on the black breast of the grave
The mother dug, and its arms full of fires.

Begin
With singing   10
Sing
Darkness kindled back into beginning
When the caught tongue nodded blind,
A star was broken
Into the centuries of the child   15
Myselves grieve now, and miracles cannot atone.

Forgive
Us forgive
Give
Us your death that myselves the believers   20
May hold it in a great flood
Till the blood shall spurt,
And the dust shall sing like a bird
As the grains blow, as your death grows, through our heart.

Crying   25
Your dying
Cry,
Child beyond cockcrow, by the fire-dwarfed
Street we chant the flying sea
In the body bereft.   30
Love is the last light spoken. Oh
Seed of sons in the loin of the black husk left.

II

I know not whether
Adam or Eve, the adorned holy bullock
Or the white ewe lamb   35
Or the chosen virgin
Laid in her snow
On the altar of London,
Was the first to die
In the cinder of the little skull,   40
O bride and bride groom
O Adam and Eve together
Lying in the lull
Under the sad breast of the head stone
White as the skeleton   45
Of the garden of Eden.

I know the legend
Of Adam and Eve is never for a second
Silent in my service
Over the dead infants   50
Over the one
Child who was priest and servants,
Word, singers, and tongue
In the cinder of the little skull,
Who was the serpent's   55
Night fall and the fruit like a sun,
Man and woman undone,
Beginning crumbled back to darkness
Bare as the nurseries
Of the garden of wilderness.   60

III

Into the organpipes and steeples
Of the luminous cathedrals,
Into the weathercocks' molten mouths
Rippling in twelve-winded circles,
Into the dead clock burning the hour   65
Over the urn of sabbaths
Over the whirling ditch of daybreak
Over the sun's hovel and the slum of fire

And the golden pavements laid in requiems,
Into the cauldrons of the statuary,   70
Into the bread in a wheatfield of flames,
Into the wine burning like brandy,
The masses of the sea
The masses of the sea under
The masses of the infant-bearing sea   75
Erupt, fountain, and enter to utter for ever
Glory glory glory
The sundering ultimate kingdom of genesis' thunder.

53

Last night I dived
my beggar arm

Last night I dived my beggar arm
Days deep in her breast that wore no heart
For me alone but only a rocked drum
Telling the heart I broke of a good habit

That her loving, unfriendly limbs   5
Would plunge my betrayal from sheet to sky
So the betrayed might learn in the sun beams
Of the death in a bed in another country.

54
Poem

Your breath was shed
Invisible to make
About the soiled undead
Night for my sake,

A raining trail   5
Intangible to them
With biter's tooth and tail
And cobweb drum,

A dark as deep
My love as a round wave   10
To hide the wolves of sleep
And mask the grave.

55
Poem in October

It was my thirtieth year to heaven
Woke to my hearing from harbour and neighbour wood
    And the mussel pooled and the heron
                Priested shore
                The morning beckon   5
With water praying and call of seagull and rook
And the knock of sailing boats on the net webbed wall
            Myself to set foot
            That second
    In the still sleeping town and set forth.   10

    My birthday began with the water-
Birds and the birds of the winged trees flying my name
    Above the farms and the white horses
                And I rose
                In rainy autumn   15

And walked abroad in a shower of all my days.
High tide and the heron dived when I took the road
    Over the border
      And the gates
Of the town closed as the town awoke.   20

  A springful of larks in a rolling
Cloud and the roadside bushes brimming with whistling
  Blackbirds and the sun of October
      Summery
      On the hill's shoulder,   25
Here were fond climates and sweet singers suddenly
Come in the morning where I wandered and listened
      To the rain wringing
      Wind blow cold
In the wood faraway under me.   30

  Pale rain over the dwindling harbour
And over the sea wet church the size of a snail
  With its horns through mist and the castle
      Brown as owls
      But all the gardens   35
Of spring and summer were blooming in the tall tales
Beyond the border and under the lark full cloud.
      There could I marvel
      My birthday
Away but the weather turned around.   40

  It turned away from the blithe country
And down the other air and the blue altered sky
  Streamed again a wonder of summer
      With apples
      Pears and red currants   45
And I saw in the turning so clearly a child's
Forgotten mornings when he walked with his mother
      Through the parables
      Of sun light
And the legends of the green chapels   50

And the twice told fields of infancy
That his tears burned my cheeks and his heart moved in mine.
These were the woods the river and sea
Where a boy
In the listening   55
Summertime of the dead whispered the truth of his joy
To the trees and the stones and the fish in the tide.
And the mystery
Sang alive
Still in the water and singingbirds.   60

And there could I marvel my birthday
Away but the weather turned around. And the true
Joy of the long dead child sang burning
In the sun.
It was my thirtieth   65
Year to heaven stood there then in the summer noon
Though the town below lay leaved with October blood.
O may my heart's truth
Still be sung
On this high hill in a year's turning.   70

56

Holy Spring

O
Out of a bed of love
When that immortal hospital made one more move to soothe
The cureless counted body,
And ruin and his causes   5
Over the barbed and shooting sea assumed an army
And swept into our wounds and houses,
I climb to greet the war in which I have no heart but only
That one dark I owe my light,
Call for confessor and wiser mirror but there is none   10

To glow after the god stoning night
And I am struck as lonely as a holy maker by the sun.

                    No
          Praise that the spring time is all
Gabriel and radiant shrubbery as the morning grows joyful   15

          Out of the woebegone pyre
And the multitude's sultry tear turns cool on the weeping wall,
          My arising prodigal
Sun the father his quiver full of the infants of pure fire,
          But blessed be hail and upheaval   20
That uncalm still it is sure alone to stand and sing
          Alone in the husk of man's home
And the mother and toppling house of the holy spring,
          If only for a last time.

57
The conversation of prayers

The conversation of prayers about to be said
By the child going to bed and the man on the stairs
Who climbs to his dying love in her high room,
The one not caring to whom in his sleep he will move
And the other full of tears that she will be dead,   5

Turns in the dark on the sound they know will arise
Into the answering skies from the green ground,
From the man on the stairs and the child by his bed.
The sound about to be said in the two prayers
For the sleep in a safe land and the love who dies   10

Will be the same grief flying. Whom shall they calm?
Shall the child sleep unharmed or the man be crying?
The conversation of prayers about to be said
Turns on the quick and the dead, and the man on the stairs
Tonight shall find no dying but alive and warm   15

In the fire of his care his love in the high room.
And the child not caring to whom he climbs his prayer
Shall drown in a grief as deep as his true grave,
And mark the dark eyed wave, through the eyes of sleep,
Dragging him up the stairs to one who lies dead.   20

58

A Refusal to Mourn the Death, by Fire, of a Child in London

Never until the mankind making
Bird beast and flower
Fathering and all humbling darkness
Tells with silence the last light breaking
And the still hour   5
Is come of the sea tumbling in harness

And I must enter again the round
Zion of the water bead
And the synagogue of the ear of corn
Shall I let pray the shadow of a sound   10
Or sow my salt seed
In the least valley of sackcloth to mourn

The majesty and burning of the child's death.
I shall not murder
The mankind of her going with a grave truth   15
Nor blaspheme down the stations of the breath
With any further
Elegy of innocence and youth.

Deep with the first dead lies London's daughter,
Robed in the long friends,   20
The grains beyond age, the dark veins of her mother,
Secret by the unmourning water
Of the riding Thames.
After the first death, there is no other.

59
This side of the truth

(for Llewelyn)

This side of the truth,
You may not see, my son,
King of your blue eyes
In the blinding country of youth,
That all is undone,   5
Under the unminding skies,
Of innocence and guilt
Before you move to make
One gesture of the heart or head,
Is gathered and spilt   10
Into the winding dark
Like the dust of the dead.

Good and bad, two ways
Of moving about your death
By the grinding sea,   15
King of your heart in the blind days,
Blow away like breath,
Go crying through you and me
And the souls of all men
Into the innocent   20
Dark, and the guilty dark, and good
Death, and bad death, and then
In the last element
Fly like the stars' blood,

Like the sun's tears,   25
Like the moon's seed, rubbish
And fire, the flying rant
Of the sky, king of your six years.
And the wicked wish,
Down the beginning of plants   30

And animals and birds,
Water and light, the earth and sky,
Is cast before you move,
And all your deeds and words,
Each truth, each lie,   35
Die in unjudging love.

60
A Winter's Tale

It is a winter's tale
That the snow blind twilight ferries over the lakes
And floating fields from the farm in the cup of the vales,
Gliding windless through the hand folded flakes,
The pale breath of cattle at the stealthy sail,   5

And the stars falling cold,
And the smell of hay in the snow, and the far owl
Warning among the folds, and the frozen hold
Flocked with the sheep white smoke of the farm house cowl
In the river wended vales where the tale was told.   10

Once when the world turned old
On a star of faith pure as the drifting bread,
As the food and flames of the snow, a man unrolled
The scrolls of fire that burned in his heart and head,
Torn and alone in a farm house in a fold   15

Of fields. And burning then
In his firelit island ringed by the winged snow
And the dung hills white as wool and the hen
Roosts sleeping chill till the flame of the cock crow
Combs through the mantled yards and the morning men   20

Stumble out with their spades,
The cattle stirring, the mousing cat stepping shy,
The puffed birds hopping and hunting, the milk maids
Gentle in their clogs over the fallen sky,
And all the woken farm at its white trades,   25

He knelt, he wept, he prayed,
By the spit and the black pot in the log bright light
And the cup and the cut bread in the dancing shade,
In the muffled house, in the quick of night,
At the point of love, forsaken and afraid. 30

He knelt on the cold stones,
He wept from the crest of grief, he prayed to the veiled sky
May his hunger go howling on bare white bones
Past the statues of the stables and the sky roofed sties
And the duck pond glass and the blinding byres alone 35

Into the home of prayers
And fires where he should prowl down the cloud
Of his snow blind love and rush in the white lairs.
His naked need struck him howling and bowed
Though no sound flowed down the hand folded air 40

But only the wind strung
Hunger of birds in the fields of the bread of water, tossed
In high corn and the harvest melting on their tongues.
And his nameless need bound him burning and lost
When cold as snow he should run the wended vales
among 45

The rivers mouthed in night,
And drown in the drifts of his need, and lie curled caught
In the always desiring centre of the white
Inhuman cradle and the bride bed forever sought
By the believer lost and the hurled outcast of light. 50

Deliver him, he cried,
By losing him all in love, and cast his need
Alone and naked in the engulfing bride,
Never to flourish in the fields of the white seed
Or flower under the time dying flesh astride. 55

Listen. The minstrels sing
In the departed villages. The nightingale,
Dust in the buried wood, flies on the grains of her wings
And spells on the winds of the dead his winter's tale.
The voice of the dust of water from the withered spring 60

Is telling. The wizened
Stream with bells and baying water bounds. The dew rings
On the gristed leaves and the long gone glistening
Parish of snow. The carved mouths in the rock are wind swept
                                                    strings.
Time sings through the intricately dead snow drop. Listen.   65

It was a hand or sound
In the long ago land that glided the dark door wide
And there outside on the bread of the ground
A she bird rose and rayed like a burning bride.
A she bird dawned, and her breast with snow and scarlet
                                                    downed.   70

Look. And the dancers move
On the departed, snow bushed green, wanton in moon light
As a dust of pigeons. Exulting, the grave hooved
Horses, centaur dead, turn and tread the drenched white
Paddocks in the farms of birds. The dead oak walks for
                                                    love.   75

The carved limbs in the rock
Leap, as to trumpets. Calligraphy of the old
Leaves is dancing. Lines of age on the stones weave in a flock.
And the harp shaped voice of the water's dust plucks in a fold
Of fields. For love, the long ago she bird rises. Look.   80

And the wild wings were raised
Above her folded head, and the soft feathered voice
Was flying through the house as though the she bird praised
And all the elements of the slow fall rejoiced
That a man knelt alone in the cup of the vales,   85

In the mantle and calm,
By the spit and the black pot in the log bright light.
And the sky of birds in the plumed voice charmed
Him up and he ran like a wind after the kindling flight
Past the blind barns and byres of the windless farm.   90

    In the poles of the year
When black birds died like priests in the cloaked hedge row
And over the cloth of counties the far hills rode near,
Under the one leaved trees ran a scarecrow of snow
And fast through the drifts of the thickets antlered like
                        deer,   95

    Rags and prayers down the knee-
Deep hillocks and loud on the numbed lakes,
All night lost and long wading in the wake of the she-
Bird through the times and lands and tribes of the slow flakes.
Listen and look where she sails the goose plucked sea,   100

    The sky, the bird, the bride,
The cloud, the need, the planted stars, the joy beyond
The fields of seed and the time dying flesh astride,
The heavens, the heaven, the grave, the burning font.
In the far ago land the door of his death glided wide,   105

    And the bird descended.
On a bread white hill over the cupped farm
And the lakes and floating fields and the river wended
Vales where he prayed to come to the last harm
And the home of prayers and fires, the tale ended.   110

    The dancing perishes
On the white, no longer growing green, and, minstrel dead,
The singing breaks in the snow shoed villages of wishes
That once cut the figures of birds on the deep bread
And over the glazed lakes skated the shapes of fishes   115

    Flying. The rite is shorn
Of nightingale and centaur dead horse. The springs wither
Back. Lines of age sleep on the stones till trumpeting dawn.
Exultation lies down. Time buries the spring weather
That belled and bounded with the fossil and the dew
                    reborn.   120

    For the bird lay bedded
In a choir of wings, as though she slept or died,
And the wings glided wide and he was hymned and wedded,
And through the thighs of the engulfing bride,
The woman breasted and the heaven headed   125

Bird, he was brought low,
Burning in the bride bed of love, in the whirl-
Pool at the wanting centre, in the folds
Of paradise, in the spun bud of the world.
And she rose with him flowering in her melting snow.   130

61
In my craft or sullen art

In my craft or sullen art
Exercised in the still night
When only the moon rages
And the lovers lie abed
With all their griefs in their arms,   5
I labour by singing light
Not for ambition or bread
Or the strut and trade of charms
On the ivory stages
But for the common wages   10
Of their most secret heart.

Not for the proud man apart
From the raging moon I write
On these spindrift pages
Nor for the towering dead   15
With their nightingales and psalms
But for the lovers, their arms
Round the griefs of the ages,
Who pay no praise or wages
Nor heed my craft or art.   20

62
Fern Hill

Now as I was young and easy under the apple boughs
About the lilting house and happy as the grass was green,
    The night above the dingle starry,
       Time let me hail and climb
    Golden in the heydays of his eyes,   5
And honoured among wagons I was prince of the apple towns
And once below a time I lordly had the trees and leaves
       Trail with daisies and barley
    Down the rivers of the windfall light.

And as I was green and carefree, famous among the barns   10
About the happy yard and singing as the farm was home,
    In the sun that is young once only,
       Time let me play and be
    Golden in the mercy of his means,
And green and golden I was huntsman and herdsman,
                   the calves   15
Sang to my horn, the foxes on the hills barked clear and cold,
       And the sabbath rang slowly
    In the pebbles of the holy streams.

All the sun long it was running, it was lovely, the hay
Fields high as the house, the tunes from the chimneys,
                  it was air   20
    And playing, lovely and watery
       And fire green as grass.
    And nightly under the simple stars
As I rode to sleep the owls were bearing the farm away,
All the moon long I heard, blessed among stables,
               the nightjars   25
    Flying with the ricks, and the horses
       Flashing into the dark.

And then to awake, and the farm, like a wanderer white
With the dew, come back, the cock on his shoulder: it was all
    Shining, it was Adam and maiden,   30

The sky gathered again
And the sun grew round that very day.
So it must have been after the birth of the simple light
In the first, spinning place, the spellbound horses walking warm
    Out of the whinnying green stable   35
        On to the fields of praise.

And honoured among foxes and pheasants by the gay house
Under the new made clouds and happy as the heart was long,
    In the sun born over and over,
        I ran my heedless ways,   40
    My wishes raced through the house high hay
And nothing I cared, at my sky blue trades, that time allows
In all his tuneful turning so few and such morning songs
    Before the children green and golden
        Follow him out of grace,   45

Nothing I cared, in the lamb white days, that time would take me
Up to the swallow thronged loft by the shadow of my hand,
    In the moon that is always rising,
        Nor that riding to sleep
    I should hear him fly with the high fields   50
And wake to the farm forever fled from the childless land.
Oh as I was young and easy in the mercy of his means,
        Time held me green and dying
    Though I sang in my chains like the sea.

63

On a Wedding Anniversary

The sky is torn across
This ragged anniversary of two
Who moved for three years in tune
Down the long walks of their vows.

Now their love lies a loss   5
And Love and his patients roar on a chain;
From every true or crater
Carrying cloud, Death strikes their house.

Too late in the wrong rain
They come together whom their love parted: 10
The windows pour into their heart
And the doors burn in their brain.

64

In Country Sleep

I

Never and never, my girl riding far and near
In the land of the hearthstone tales, and spelled asleep,
Fear or believe that the wolf in a sheepwhite hood
Loping and bleating roughly and blithely shall leap,
          My dear, my dear,   5
Out of a lair in the flocked leaves in the dew dipped year
To eat your heart in the house in the rosy wood.

Sleep, good, for ever, slow and deep, spelled rare and wise,
My girl ranging the night in the rose and shire
Of the hobnail tales: no gooseherd or swine will turn   10
Into a homestall king or hamlet of fire
          And prince of ice
To court the honeyed heart from your side before sunrise
In a spinney of ringed boys and ganders, spike and burn,

Nor the innocent lie in the rooting dingle wooed   15
And staved, and riven among plumes my rider weep.
From the broomed witch's spume you are shielded by fern
And flower of country sleep and the greenwood keep.
          Lie fast and soothed,
Safe be and smooth from the bellows of the rushy brood.   20

Never, my girl, until tolled to sleep by the stern

Bell believe or fear that the rustic shade or spell
Shall harrow and snow the blood while you ride wide and near,
For who unmanningly haunts the mountain ravened eaves
Or skulks in the dell moon but moonshine echoing clear   25
                  From the starred well?
A hill touches an angel. Out of a saint's cell
The nightbird lauds through nunneries and domes of leaves

Her robin breasted tree, three Marys in the rays.
Sanctum sanctorum the animal eye of the wood   30
In the rain telling its beads, and the gravest ghost
The owl at its knelling. Fox and holt kneel before blood.
                  Now the tales praise
The star rise at pasture and nightlong the fables graze
On the lord's table of the bowing grass. Fear most   35

For ever of all not the wolf in his baaing hood
Nor the tusked prince, in the ruttish farm, at the rind
And mire of love, but the Thief as meek as the dew.
The country is holy: O bide in that country kind,
                  Know the green good,   40
Under the prayer wheeling moon in the rosy wood
Be shielded by chant and flower and gay may you

Lie in grace. Sleep spelled at rest in the lowly house
In the squirrel nimble grove, under linen and thatch
And star: held and blessed, though you scour the high four   45
Winds, from the dousing shade and the roarer at the latch,
                  Cool in your vows.
Yet out of the beaked, web dark and the pouncing boughs
Be you sure the Thief will seek a way sly and sure

And sly as snow and meek as dew blown to the thorn,   50
This night and each vast night until the stern bell talks
In the tower and tolls to sleep over the stalls
Of the hearthstone tales my own, last love; and the soul walks
                  The waters shorn.
This night and each night since the falling star you were
                    born,   55

Ever and ever he finds a way, as the snow falls,

As the rain falls, hail on the fleece, as the vale mist rides
Through the haygold stalls, as the dew falls on the wind-
Milled dust of the apple tree and the pounded islands
Of the morning leaves, as the star falls, as the winged   60
                    Apple seed glides,
And falls, and flowers in the yawning wound at our sides,
As the world falls, silent as the cyclone of silence.

                    II

Night and the reindeer on the clouds above the haycocks
And the wings of the great roc ribboned for the fair!   65
The leaping saga of prayer! And high, there, on the hare-
                    Heeled winds the rooks
Cawing from their black bethels soaring, the holy books
Of birds! Among the cocks like fire the red fox

Burning! Night and the vein of birds in the winged,
                    sloe wrist   70
Of the wood! Pastoral beat of blood through the laced leaves!
The stream from the priest black wristed spinney and sleeves
                    Of thistling frost
Of the nightingale's din and tale! The upgiven ghost
Of the dingle torn to singing and the surpliced   75

Hill of cypresses! The din and tale in the skimmed
Yard of the buttermilk rain on the pail! The sermon
Of blood! The bird loud vein! The saga from mermen
                    To seraphim
Leaping! The gospel rooks! All tell, this night, of him   80
Who comes as red as the fox and sly as the heeled wind.

Illumination of music! the lulled black backed
Gull, on the wave with sand in its eyes! And the foal moves
Through the shaken greensward lake, silent, on moonshod hooves,
                    In the winds' wakes.   85
Music of elements, that a miracle makes!
Earth, air, water, fire, singing into the white act,

The haygold haired, my love asleep, and the rift blue
Eyed, in the haloed house, in her rareness and hilly
High riding, held and blessed and true, and so stilly   90

Lying the sky
Might cross its planets, the bell weep, night gather her eyes,
The Thief fall on the dead like the willynilly dew,

Only for the turning of the earth in her holy
Heart! Slyly, slowly, hearing the wound in her side go   95
Round the sun, he comes to my love like the designed snow,
And truly he
Flows to the strand of flowers like the dew's ruly sea,
And surely he sails like the ship shape clouds. Oh he

Comes designed to my love to steal not her tide raking   100
Wound, nor her riding high, nor her eyes, nor kindled hair,
But her faith that each vast night and the saga of prayer
He comes to take
Her faith that this last night for his unsacred sake
He comes to leave her in the lawless sun awaking   105

Naked and forsaken to grieve he will not come.
Ever and ever by all your vows believe and fear
My dear this night he comes and night without end my dear
Since you were born:
And you shall wake, from country sleep, this dawn and each
first dawn,   110

Your faith as deathless as the outcry of the ruled sun.

65
Over Sir John's hill

Over Sir John's hill,
The hawk on fire hangs still;
In a hoisted cloud, at drop of dusk, he pulls to his claws
And gallows, up the rays of his eyes the small birds of the bay
And the shrill child's play   5

Wars
Of the sparrows and such who swansing, dusk, in wrangling
                                        hedges.
And blithely they squawk
To fiery tyburn over the wrestle of elms until
The flash the noosed hawk   10
Crashes, and slowly the fishing holy stalking heron
In the river Towy below bows his tilted headstone.

Flash, and the plumes crack,
And a black cap of jack-
Daws Sir John's just hill dons, and again the gulled birds
                                        hare   15
To the hawk on fire, the halter height, over Towy's fins,
In a whack of wind.
There
Where the elegiac fisherbird stabs and paddles
In the pebbly dab filled   20
Shallow and sedge, and 'dilly dilly,' calls the loft hawk,
'Come and be killed,'
I open the leaves of the water at a passage
Of psalms and shadows among the pincered sandcrabs prancing

And read, in a shell,   25
Death clear as a buoy's bell:
All praise of the hawk on fire in hawk-eyed dusk be sung,
When his viperish fuse hangs looped with flames under the
                                        brand
Wing, and blest shall
Young   30
Green chickens of the bay and bushes cluck, 'dilly dilly,
Come let us die.'
We grieve as the blithe birds, never again, leave shingle and elm,
The heron and I,
I young Aesop fabling to the near night by the dingle   35
Of eels, saint heron hymning in the shell-hung distant

Crystal harbour vale
Where the sea cobbles sail,
And wharves of water where the walls dance and the white
                                        cranes stilt.
It is the heron and I, under judging Sir John's elmed   40

Hill, tell-tale the knelled
Guilt
Of the led-astray birds whom God, for their breast of whistles,
Have mercy on,
God in his whirlwind silence save, who marks the sparrows
                                                                        hail,   45
For their souls' song.
Now the heron grieves in the weeded verge. Through windows
Of dusk and water I see the tilting whispering

Heron, mirrored, go,
As the snapt feathers snow,   50
Fishing in the tear of the Towy. Only a hoot owl
Hollows, a grassblade blown in cupped hands, in the looted
                                                                        elms,
And no green cocks or hens
Shout
Now on Sir John's hill. The heron, ankling the scaly   55
Lowlands of the waves,
Makes all the music; and I who hear the tune of the slow,
Wear-willow river, grave,
Before the lunge of the night, the notes on this time-shaken
Stone for the sake of the souls of the slain birds sailing.   60

66

In the White Giant's Thigh

Through throats where many rivers meet, the curlews cry,
Under the conceiving moon, on the high chalk hill,
And there this night I walk in the white giant's thigh
Where barren as boulders women lie longing still

To labour and love though they lay down long ago.   5

Through throats where many rivers meet, the women pray,
Pleading in the waded bay for the seed to flow
Though the names on their weed grown stones are rained away,

And alone in the night's eternal, curving act
They yearn with tongues of curlews for the unconceived   10
And immemorial sons of the cudgelling, hacked

Hill. Who once in gooseskin winter loved all ice leaved
In the courters' lanes, or twined in the ox roasting sun
In the wains tonned so high that the wisps of the hay
Clung to the pitching clouds, or gay with anyone   15
Young as they in the after milking moonlight lay

Under the lighted shapes of faith and their moonshade
Petticoats galed high, or shy with the rough riding boys,
Now clasp me to their grains in the gigantic glade,

Who once, green countries since, were a hedgerow of joys.   20

Time by, their dust was flesh the swineherd rooted sly,
Flared in the reek of the wiving sty with the rush
Light of his thighs, spreadeagle to the dunghill sky,
Or with their orchard man in the core of the sun's bush
Rough as cows' tongues and thrashed with brambles their
                                        buttermilk   25
Manes, under his quenchless summer barbed gold to the bone,

Or rippling soft in the spinney moon as the silk
And ducked and draked white lake that harps to a hail stone.

Who once were a bloom of wayside brides in the hawed house
And heard the lewd, wooed field flow to the coming frost,   30
The scurrying, furred small friars squeal, in the dowse
Of day, in the thistle aisles, till the white owl crossed

Their breast, the vaulting does roister, the horned bucks climb
Quick in the wood at love, where a torch of foxes foams,
All birds and beasts of the linked night uproar and chime   35

And the mole snout blunt under his pilgrimage of domes,

Or, butter fat goosegirls, bounced in a gambo bed,
Their breasts full of honey, under their gander king
Trounced by his wings in the hissing shippen, long dead
And gone that barley dark where their clogs danced in the
                                        spring,   40
And their firefly hairpins flew, and the ricks ran round –

(But nothing bore, no mouthing babe to the veined hives
Hugged, and barren and bare on Mother Goose's ground
They with the simple Jacks were a boulder of wives) –
Now curlew cry me down to kiss the mouths of their dust.   45

The dust of their kettles and clocks swings to and fro
Where the hay rides now or the bracken kitchens rust
As the arc of the billhooks that flashed the hedges low
And cut the birds' boughs that the minstrel sap ran red.
They from houses where the harvest kneels, hold me hard,   50
Who heard the tall bell sail down the Sundays of the dead
And the rain wring out its tongues on the faded yard,
Teach me the love that is evergreen after the fall leaved
Grave, after Beloved on the grass gulfed cross is scrubbed
Off by the sun and Daughters no longer grieved   55
Save by their long desirers in the fox cubbed
Streets or hungering in the crumbled wood: to these
Hale dead and deathless do the women of the hill
Love forever meridian through the courters' trees

And the daughters of darkness flame like Fawkes fires still.   60

67
Lament

When I was a windy boy and a bit
And the black spit of the chapel fold,
(Sighed the old ram rod, dying of women),
I tiptoed shy in the gooseberry wood,
The rude owl cried like a telltale tit,   5
I skipped in a blush as the big girls rolled
Ninepin down on the donkeys' common,
And on seesaw sunday nights I wooed
Whoever I would with my wicked eyes,
The whole of the moon I could love and leave   10
All the green leaved little weddings' wives
In the coal black bush and let them grieve.

When I was a gusty man and a half
And the black beast of the beetles' pews,
(Sighed the old ram rod, dying of bitches),   15

Not a boy and a bit in the wick-
Dipping moon and drunk as a new dropped calf,
I whistled all night in the twisted flues,
Midwives grew in the midnight ditches,
And the sizzling beds of the town cried, Quick! –   20
Whenever I dove in a breast high shoal,
Wherever I ramped in the clover quilts,
Whatsoever I did in the coal-
Black night, I left my quivering prints.

When I was a man you could call a man   25
And the black cross of the holy house,
(Sighed the old ram rod, dying of welcome),
Brandy and ripe in my bright, bass prime,
No springtailed tom in the red hot town
With every simmering woman his mouse   30
But a hillocky bull in the swelter
Of summer come in his great good time
To the sultry, biding herds, I said,
Oh, time enough when the blood creeps cold,
And I lie down but to sleep in bed,   35
For my sulking, skulking, coal black soul!

When I was a half of the man I was
And serve me right as the preachers warn,
(Sighed the old ram rod, dying of downfall),
No flailing calf or cat in a flame   40
Or hickory bull in milky grass
But a black sheep with a crumpled horn,
At last the soul from its foul mousehole
Slunk pouting out when the limp time came;
And I gave my soul a blind, slashed eye,   45
Gristle and rind, and a roarer's life,
And I shoved it into the coal black sky
To find a woman's soul for a wife.

Now I am a man no more no more
And a black reward for a roaring life,   50

(Sighed the old ram rod, dying of strangers),
Tidy and cursed in my dove cooed room
I lie down thin and hear the good bells jaw –
For, oh, my soul found a sunday wife
In the coal black sky and she bore angels!　　55
Harpies around me out of her womb!
Chastity prays for me, piety sings,
Innocence sweetens my last black breath,
Modesty hides my thighs in her wings,
And all the deadly virtues plague my death!　　60

68
Do not go gentle into that good night

Do not go gentle into that good night,
Old age should burn and rave at close of day;
Rage, rage against the dying of the light.

Though wise men at their end know dark is right,
Because their words had forked no lightning they　　5
Do not go gentle into that good night.

Good men, the last wave by, crying how bright
Their frail deeds might have danced in a green bay,
Rage, rage against the dying of the light.

Wild men who caught and sang the sun in flight,　　10
And learn, too late, they grieved it on its way,
Do not go gentle into that good night.

Grave men, near death, who see with blinding sight
Blind eyes could blaze like meteors and be gay,
Rage, rage against the dying of the light.　　15

And you, my father, there on the sad height,
Curse, bless, me now with your fierce tears, I pray,
Do not go gentle into that good night.
Rage, rage against the dying of the light.

69
Poem on his Birthday

In the mustardseed sun,
By full tilt river and switchback sea
  Where the cormorants scud,
In his house on stilts high among beaks
  And palavers of birds   5
This sandgrain day in the bent bay's grave
  He celebrates and spurns
His driftwood thirty-fifth wind turned age;
  Herons spire and spear.

  Under and round him go   10
Flounders, gulls, on their cold, dying trails,
  Doing what they are told,
Curlews aloud in the congered waves
  Work at their ways to death,
And the rhymer in the long tongued room,   15
  Who tolls his birthday bell,
Toils towards the ambush of his wounds;
  Herons, steeple stemmed, bless.

  In the thistledown fall,
He sings towards anguish; finches fly   20
  In the claw tracks of hawks
On a seizing sky; small fishes glide
  Through wynds and shells of drowned
Ship towns to pastures of otters. He
  In his slant, racking house   25
And the hewn coils of his trade perceives
  Herons walk in their shroud,

  The livelong river's robe
Of minnows wreathing around their prayer;
  And far at sea he knows,   30

Who slaves to his crouched, eternal end
  Under a serpent cloud,
Dolphins dive in their turnturtle dust,
  The rippled seals streak down
To kill and their own tide daubing blood   35
  Slides good in the sleek mouth.

  In a cavernous, swung
Wave's silence, wept white angelus knells.
  Thirty-five bells sing struck
On skull and scar where his loves lie wrecked,   40
  Steered by the falling stars.
And tomorrow weeps in a blind cage
  Terror will rage apart
Before chains break to a hammer flame
  And love unbolts the dark   45

  And freely he goes lost
In the unknown, famous light of great
  And fabulous, dear God.
Dark is a way and light is a place,
  Heaven that never was   50
Nor will be ever is always true,
  And, in that brambled void,
Plenty as blackberries in the woods
  The dead grow for His joy.

  There he might wander bare   55
With the spirits of the horseshoe bay
  Or the stars' seashore dead,
Marrow of eagles, the roots of whales
  And wishbones of wild geese,
With blessed, unborn God and His Ghost,   60
  And every soul His priest,
Gulled and chanter in young Heaven's fold
  Be at cloud quaking peace,

  But dark is a long way.
He, on the earth of the night, alone   65

With all the living, prays,
Who knows the rocketing wind will blow
      The bones out of the hills,
And the scythed boulders bleed, and the last
      Rage shattered waters kick   70
Masts and fishes to the still quick stars,
      Faithlessly unto Him

      Who is the light of old
And air shaped Heaven where souls grow wild
      As horses in the foam: 75
Oh, let me midlife mourn by the shrined
      And druid herons' vows
The voyage to ruin I must run,
      Dawn ships clouted aground,
Yet, though I cry with tumbledown tongue,   80
      Count my blessings aloud:

      Four elements and five
Senses, and man a spirit in love
      Tangling through this spun slime
To his nimbus bell cool kingdom come   85
      And the lost, moonshine domes,
And the sea that hides his secret selves
      Deep in its black, base bones,
Lulling of spheres in the seashell flesh,
      And this last blessing most,   90

      That the closer I move
To death, one man through his sundered hulks,
      The louder the sun blooms
And the tusked, ramshackling sea exults;
      And every wave of the way   95
And gale I tackle, the whole world then
      With more triumphant faith
Than ever was since the world was said
      Spins its morning of praise,

      I hear the bouncing hills   100

Grow larked and greener at berry brown
   Fall and the dew larks sing
Taller this thunderclap spring, and how
   More spanned with angels ride
The mansouled fiery islands! Oh,   105
   Holier then their eyes,
And my shining men no more alone
   As I sail out to die.

70

Elegy

Too proud to die, broken and blind he died
The darkest way, and did not turn away,
A cold, kind man brave in his burning pride

On that darkest day. Oh, forever may
He live lightly, at last, on the last, crossed   5
Hill, and there grow young, under the grass, in love,

Among the long flocks, and never lie lost
Or still all the days of his death, though above
All he longed all dark for his mother's breast

Which was rest and dust, and in the kind ground   10
The darkest justice of death, blind and unblessed.
Let him find no rest but be fathered and found,

I prayed in the crouching room, by his blind bed,
In the muted house, one minute before
Noon, and night, and light. The rivers of the dead   15

Moved in his poor hand I held, and I saw
Through his faded eyes to the roots of the sea.
Go calm to your crucified hill, I told

The air that drew away from him.

NOTES

1 Prologue (August 1952)

Written specially for *Collected Poems*, 1952. In a letter (10 September 1952) Thomas wrote: "I hope the Prologue *does* read as a prologue, and not as just another poem. I think – though I am too near it now to be any judge – that it *does* do what it sets out to do: addresses the readers, the 'strangers', with a flourish and fanfare, and makes clear, or tries to make clear, the position of one writer in a world 'at poor peace'." The Prologue ("this rumpus of shapes", l.37) dedicates the *Collected Poems* ("these seathumbed leaves", 1.29).

The first and last lines rhyme, and so on inwards until the exact centre of the poem (lines 51 and 52) is a rhyming couplet.

ll.19–20 THE CITIES OF NINE/DAYS' NIGHT: the poet mixes two references to describe, mainly, London where he made his poetic and personal reputations: 'The City of Dreadful Night' and the proverbial phrase 'A nine days' wonder'.

l.33 DOGDAYED: 'Dog-days', named after the Dog-star, are the hottest days of the year, early July to middle August.

l.44 BELLOWING ARK: the sustained idea of Noah's Ark is an image of Thomas 'building' his poems as an act of survival.

l.56 DEER: the old sense of 'beasts', 'animals'. Cf. *King Lear*, III, 4, 135 : 'mice and rats and such small deer.'

l.57 BRYNS: Welsh for 'hills'.

2 The spire cranes (*Notebook* version January 1931)

Compare Thomas's *Once it was the colour of saying* and *On no work of words*.

The spire is an image of the poet. The stone birds carved in the masonry stand for those poems which, because they are either too artificially made or too private in their meaning, fail to escape into communication with the outside world. In contrast, the chimes and the real living birds suggest a more vital and communicating kind of poetry, because they escape from the poet-spire.

Line 6 is the only exception to a syllabic count of 12 in each line.

ll.2–3 THE FEATHERY/CARVED BIRDS: the carved birds are covered with the moulted feathers of the real birds. Regarding the "carved birds", cf. Thomas's remark in a letter (answering a criticism by Stephen Spender) "My poems *are* formed; they are not turned on like a tap at all ... the last thing they do is to flow; they are much rather hewn".

l.4 THE SPILT SKY: the sea.

l.6 THAT PRIEST, WATER: cf. Keats's 'Bright star' sonnet – 'waters at their priestlike task/ Of pure ablution round earth's human shores.'

ll.7–8 SILVER LOCK/ AND MOUTH suggest the singing voice.

ll.9–11 The more artificial, private poems pose a problem of choice for the poet. Should he stop writing them? As they stand, they communicate only backwards to the poet himself. They do not get soiled and tested in the real world (like the Prodigal Son) before returning.

3 Being but men (*Notebook* only, May 1932)

4 Out of the sighs (*Notebook* version June–July 1932)

Compare Emily Dickinson's "After great pain, a formal feeling comes ..." and her "'Tis so much joy! 'tis so much joy", and Thomas Hardy's *In Tenebris*, part I.

Perhaps as a first entry into this poem the reader would do well to hold quite literally to the idea of disappointment in love; but it will also be seen that the poem registers a disaffection with life in general. Either way, the main emphasis is on a stoic realism about life's possibilities.

ll.1–4 The speaker has made a decision against holding a tragic view of life ("grief", "agony"). By giving in only to "sighs", he at least keeps himself open to a few cold comforts.

ll.7–9 The elliptical syntax can be opened out thus: 'There must, [God] be praised, [be] some certainty, if not [the certainty] of loving well, then [that of] not [loving well] ...'

ll.10–11 Cf. 'Cowards die many times before their deaths'.

ll.12–16 *General sense*: 'Even if someone eased the pain of the experience of parting, the ache continues because of the realization that regret which can be thus easily remedied is no regret at all.' ("Through no regret" here means 'because there is no regret'.)

ll.17–24 *General sense*: 'If mere regret after lost happiness could *completely* "ease the pain", or if 'vague' words and "lies" could do it, the speaker would willingly join in the hypocrisy of "hollow words".

ll.25–28 *General sense*: 'If such remedies *were* completely adequate, it would suggest that man was as easily satisfied as a dog.'

ll.29–30 Man and his situation being more complicated than that, the speaker at least *recognizes* and *accepts* his dog's life! – its "crumbs" (meagre rewards), "barn" (poverty, imprisonment) and "halter" (tying-rope, noose).

5 Out of a war of wits (*Notebook* only, February 1933)

Around this time, Thomas and his friends used to meet regularly on Wednesday evenings at the poet's home in Swansea, for discussions and arguments which went on late into the night.

6 Their faces shone under some radiance
(*Notebook* only, February 1933)

Compare Thomas Hardy's *Beyond the Last Lamp* (*Near Tooting Common*). At one stage Thomas's poem had the subtitle "In Hyde Park".

7 I have longed to move away (*Notebook* version March 1933)

Compare Philip Larkin's *Wants* and *Poetry of Departures*.
The speaker wishes to escape from social and religious conventions, which he considers bogus and hypocritical. But the thought worries him (lines 11–14) that convention, even if false, is nevertheless a form of security whereby the individual has at least company in facing the unknown, a kind of safety in numbers.

l.2 THE HISSING OF THE SPENT LIE suggests the serpent of *Genesis*, as well as the primary metaphor of a firework.

l.3 OLD TERRORS: the fears and superstitions on which society thrives.

l.7 SALUTES: apart from the military sense of discipline, the ordinary social courtesies, parodies of communication.

ll.8–9 One reason for wanting to escape is that conventional superstition ("ghosts in the air") is also dictating the attitudes of his poetry ("ghostly echoes on paper").

l.10 CALLS AND NOTES: apart from the military (and religious) idea of a trumpet sounding, there is the simpler notion of telephone-calls and visiting-cards (see line 17 below).

ll.15–18 The irony is that man, in any case, doesn't die from his superstitions and fears; whether he conventionally suffers from them or not, it is only death which kills him!

l.16 THE PARTING OF HAT FROM HAIR: the idea of hair standing on end (fright), and a repetition of the idea of social courtesy – a gentleman lifts his hat to ladies!

l.17 RECEIVER: telephone-receiver.

ll.19–20 *a* He 'would not mind' dying of these since, being bogus, they would make death itself unreal; but *b* neither 'would he choose to' let these obscure a more real sense of life and death.

8 And death shall have no dominion (*Notebook* version April 1933)

Compare Donne's Holy Sonnet "Death be not proud …", Shelley's *Adonais*, stanzas 39–44, and Thomas's *A Refusal to Mourn the Death, by Fire, of a Child in London*.

l.1 This repeated line is based on a clause in St Paul's Epistle to the Romans (vi. 9): "Christ being raised from the dead dieth no more; death hath no more dominion over him." And lines 7 and 11–12 remind us of *Revelation* (xx. 13): "And the sea gave up the dead which were in it." But Thomas's poem is more pantheistic than Christian. What it affirms is the indissolubility of the general fact and principle of Life, not any promise of individual Christian resurrection.

l.3 A juggled reference to the man in the moon and the west wind.

l.12 WINDILY: mainly 'in vain'; but a slang meaning would also seem appropriate – 'in a state of fright'. The word has been brought to mind by "windings" in the previous line.

ll.13–18 These lines suggest the death of martyrs (St Catherine was tortured and killed on a spiked wheel). Even if their faith gives way, the defeat of an ideology is never the end of life itself.

l.16 UNICORN EVILS: the phrase suggests both the brutalities of torture and the rending spiritual pains involved in a loss of faith.

ll.19–23 Natural phenomena – the cry of gulls, the sound of the sea, a flower – in a sense owe their existence to the human perception which recognizes and appreciates them. If one judges merely from the viewpoint of an individual, the natural world would appear to die when the individual dies. Individuality dies, but general cosmic life continues.

l.25 Cf. the euphemism 'Pushing up daisies'. "Hammer" was suggested by "nails" in the previous line.

l.26 BREAK: break open (with the flowers).

9 We lying by seasand (*Notebook* version May 1933)

10 Ears in the turrets hear (*Notebook* version July 1933)

Compare section V and VI of Yeats's *Meditations in Time of Civil War*, and Louis MacNeice's *Prognosis*.

"And living in your own private, four-walled world as exclusively as possible isn't escapism, I'm sure; it isn't the Ivory Tower, and, even if it were, you secluded in your Tower know and learn more of the world outside than the outside-man who is mixed up so personally and inextricably with the mud and the unlovely people" (Thomas in a letter to Vernon Watkins). This poem is about the self-absorption of Thomas the man and the private nature of his poetic world. It shows his fear and uncertainty in recognizing that 'No man is an island unto himself'.

11 Here in this spring (*Notebook* version July 1933)

In nature, impressions of beauty and growth coexist with signs of death.

ll.1–4 Mixed in with conventional associations ("spring", "*ornamental* winter") are darker indications of extinction and suffering – the stars float in a "void", and line 3 reminds us of the storm in *King Lear*. Even summer, the height of life and growth, is a death – of spring.

l.3 Puns on "down" (= feathers = snow) and "pelts" (= animal skins) give a secondary meaning to the line – 'down-like snow clothes the naked weather'.

ll.7–8 The implication is that while, on the one hand, autumn fruitfulness makes us think of only "three seasons" (spring, summer and autumn itself), autumn's decay reminds us that it takes winter to complete the full cycle of four.

l.9 I SHOULD TELL: 'I would think it' summer if I looked only at the trees.

l.12 I SHOULD LEARN: 'I would expect' spring if I listened only to the cuckoo which heralds it.

l.14 BETTER: 'more truthfully', because the worm also tells us that summer will pass.

l.16 WHAT SHALL IT TELL ME: 'What exactly is the significance of the message that the world wears away, and what the responsibilities that go along with knowing it?'

12 Why east wind chills (*Notebook* version July 1933)

Compare Robert Frost's *Neither Out Far Nor In Deep* and his *The Most Of It*, Robert Graves's *Warning to Children* and Thomas's *Should lanterns shine* and *This Side of the Truth*.

The theme is man's necessary ignorance of any final answers in the face of a mysterious universe.

l.1 The basic futility of the questions makes fun of man's tendency to seek intellectual explanations of natural mysteries. However, the questions also evoke the dialogue and catechism form of certain medieval texts designed for instructive reading, which Thomas may have met in Shakespeare (eg. *King Lear* I, 5, 27 and 34 and III, 4, 152.)

l.2 WINDWELL: the source of the winds, something like Aeolus's cave of winds in classical mythology.

l.10 COMETH: the archaic form makes the question appear both quaint and timeless.

JACK FROST suggests on the one hand innocent winter magic and, on the other, Death.

l.11 The "comet" represents an answer to a metaphysical question. The image is borrowed from John Donne's *Song* "Go, and catch a falling star ..."

FISTS: clenched hands suggest defiance and frustration where a more relaxed receptivity should be.

ll.16–20 "All things are known" is ironically intended. Astrology ("the stars' advice") gives some people a false confidence that they are in league with the mysterious order of things. But only the end of the world will show how much the stars themselves are ignorant of!

l.19 TOWERS: originally Thomas had written "houses", suggesting that he means the various stations of the Zodiac.

l.21 CONTENT: both noun (*content*ment) and adverb (*content*edly).

13 The hand that signed the paper (*Notebook* version August 1933)

Compare W. H. Auden's *Epitaph on a Tyrant*.

Thomas on the whole resisted the fashion of his generation for 'political' and 'socially conscious' poetry. This is the only poem in *Collected Poems* to be on an overtly political subject. In its *Notebook* version it was dedicated to Bert Trick, an early Swansea friend and an active member of the left wing of the Labour Party.

With one exception (line 4) the stanzas are regularly syllabic – 11, 8, 11, 6.

l.2 SOVEREIGN: the proximity of "taxed" gives "sovereign" its monetary as well as its regal meaning.

l.4 FIVE KINGS: five fingers.

A KING: Christ may be suggested, as well as any ordinary, political king.

ll.5–6. The irony of "mighty" is driven home by references to the tyrant's "sloping shoulder" and his hand "cramped with chalk", which suggests both writer's cramp and arthritis.

ll.7–8. The two uses of "put an end to" have different meanings: 'a signature has as good as *accomplished* murder, which *put an end* to protest'.

l.15 The comparison with "heaven" and God has been led up to by the suggestion of the Old Testament in the previous stanza ("famine", "locusts").

14 That sanity be kept (1933)

Compare T. S. Eliot's *Morning at the Window*.

"The more I think of my ... poem the less I like it. The idea of myself sitting in the open window, in my shirt, and imagining myself as some Jehovah of the West, is really odd. If I were some Apollo it would be different" (letter to Pamela Hansford Johnson).

15 Before I knocked (*Notebook* version September 1933)

The speaker's consciousness predates, not only birth, but conception itself. Several hints in the poem make us think of that speaker as being Christ. But knowing how often Thomas fuses his own and everyman's identity with Christ, we can equally well take the primary speaker to be the poet, mythologized by analogies with Christ.

The poem has an unbroken syllabic count – lines of 9 and 8 syllables alternating throughout.

l.5 MNETHA: a name Thomas remembered from Blake's *Tiriel*. Mnetha's daughter was Heva, portrayed by Blake as sharing kinship with all things. Thomas would have been equally intrigued by 'Mnetha's' role as anagram – of 'anthem', 'the man', or 'Athena(m)'.

ll.23–24 The words "gallow crosses" and "brambles" suggest the crucifixion.

l.39 DEATH'S FEATHER: cf. John Donne (*Devotions*): "There is scarce anything that hath not killed some body; a hair, a feather hath done it." But Thomas is equally likely to have been using the common expression 'You could have knocked me down with a feather'.

l.44 REMEMBER ME AND PITY HIM: Thomas is possibly suggesting that Christ was not, in the nature of things, able to fulfil Himself physically.

l.46 DOUBLECROSSED: *a* 'crossed twice' (God was both Father and Son in the Incarnation); *b* 'betrayed' (the idea that Christ may not have been the Son of God, as promised to Mary); *c* caused Mary to suffer twice – in the pain of birth and at Christ's later crucifixion.

It will be noticed, though, that Thomas writes "*my* mother's womb".

The manuscript version, however, read "*his* mother's womb". If not a simple error, "my" may have been used to suggest *a* that *every* birth is an Incarnation, and *b* that Christ's birth doublecrosses or betrays every secular birth by establishing the inadequacy of a merely physical interpretation of life.

16 My hero bears his nerves (*Notebook* version September 1933)

Compare Ted Hughes's *The Thought-Fox* and Thomas's *In my craft or sullen art*

The poem is an elaborate conceit. On one level it evokes the physical act of writing: the "nerves" and "head" of the poet's sensibility and mind are 'unpacked' in an "unruly scrawl" onto the "lovelorn paper" etc. The final line ("He pulls the chain, the cistern moves") and the mechanistic images throughout draw an analogy between this cathartic act of writing and the flushing of an old-fashioned water-closet. An additional analogy in the metaphors is with masturbation (another *Notebook* poem of the same year contains the phrase "cistern sex").

l.12 NAKED VENUS: an image wittily comparing the heart, with its emerging veins and arteries, to the heart-shaped face and red plaits of Botticelli's famous 'The Birth of Venus', a favourite painting of the poet's.

17 Song ("Love me, not as the dreaming nurses ...")
(*Notebook* version September 1933)

18 The force that through the green fuse
(*Notebook* version October 1933)

The identification of the world's elemental forces with those which
govern the human body, so characteristic of Thomas's poetry, is in itself
clear enough. A greater difficulty would seem to lie in the repeated "And
I am dumb to tell ..." Thomas is possibly emphasizing the irony that,
though physically man is one with the universe, he is separated from it
by intellectual consciousness. In other words, the lament is not that he is
dumb to tell, but that he can conceive of *telling* in the first place. In that
sense, "dumb to tell" also means 'foolish to tell'.

l.2 BLASTS: not just 'blows on', but 'explodes' (see 'fuse', l.1).
l.4 CROOKED ROSE: along with the "crooked worm" of the poem's final
    line, it suggests Blake's *The Sick Rose*.
l.12 QUICKSAND: apart from the obvious meaning, there is possibly a
    reference to sand pouring quickly through an hour-glass, and a pun on
    'quick' = living.
l.14 The "hanging man", being dead, is now genuinely one with the
    merely physical world to which the poet is dumb to tell.
l.15 HANGMAN'S LIME: the *quick*lime used to destroy the bodies of
    executed criminals buried in it.
l.16 THE FOUNTAIN HEAD: apart from the literal meaning, a metaphor for
    the womb from which time "sucks" the newly born.
l.20 The line suggests that, under the pressure of Time, man has invented
    Eternity – ticking a heaven round the stars, just as a clock's hands,
    moving from hour to hour, ticks a perfect circle on the clock face.
l.22 Apart from the primary meaning of bedsheet and winding sheet, the
    "crooked worm" is possibly also the poet's finger moving on the 'sheet'
    of paper on which the poem is written.

19 Light breaks where no sun shines
(*Notebook* version November 1933)

Compare *When all my five and country senses see*.
"My own obscurity ... is ... based on a preconceived symbolism derived
from the cosmic significance of the human anatomy" (Thomas in a letter).
Here Thomas not so much compares as *identifies* the human body with
the physical universe – an identification which elementalizes the body and
personalizes the universe.
    Only the penultimate line of the whole poem interrupts a regular
syllabic count of 6, 10, 4, 10, 4, 10 in each stanza.
    The following stanza-by-stanza paraphrase acts only as a guideline. It

has had to avoid additional suggestions and alternative meanings at certain points.

Stanza One: (ll.1–3) In the formed body, consciousness dawns like light, blood moves like a sea; (ll.4–6) two *simultaneous* meanings – at conception, light itself creates the flesh, and after death worms move through the earth which now *is* the flesh around the bones.

Stanza Two: (ll.7–8) In the formed body, the sexual organs produce sperm, and destroy the sperm which is unused; (ll.9–11) before birth, the embryo uncurls like any fact of physical creation; (l.12) after death, when ordinary growth (pun on "wax") has ceased, the sexual organ is denuded like a candle of its wax.

Stanza Three: (ll.13–15) In the formed body, consciousness dawns like light, blood moves like a sea; (ll.16–18) and because the universe is not different or separate (not "fenced" or "staked") rain is the same response to that process which 'divines' (discovers and makes holy) tears of grief behind a human smile.

Stanza Four: (ll.1–3) Sleep presages Death by darkening the eyes (a reminder also of the *limit*ations of ordinary eyesight); and as sight in daytime shows the body, *in*sight reveals the bone; (ll.22–24) after death, the flesh, like winter earth, is laid bare – but notions of warm and cold have ceased to matter; the thin thread which will produce spring growth is now literally fixed to the corpse's eyelid, corporate but unseen (pun on "film").

Stanza Five: After death, a *new* consciousness emerges, nothing to do with intellect, and in which abstract 'thought' becomes physical sense, in which the mystery of growth, no longer an idea, is an actual growth in the skeleton's eyesockets, and in which blood vitalizes the plants responding to sunshine, life's source; (l.30) after this new organic consciousness, there is no other: "the dawn halts".

20 A Letter to my Aunt Discussing the Correct Approach to Modern Poetry (December 1933)

This was included in a letter to Pamela Hansford Johnson. In itself, of course, it is a mere sport. But it serves as a useful reminder of Thomas's sense of humour and his mistrust of poetical 'fashions' or critical piety where poetry was concerned.

l.8 "David G." is David Gascoyne, the Surrealist poet.

21 This bread I break (*Notebook* version December 1933)

The poet's main emphasis is on the irony (pinpointed in the pun on "break") that the bread and wine which signify and give Christ's *life* in the Holy Communion are made from the *death* of nature. Characteristically, the poem resists man's tendency to abstract significance from an already significant (because vital) world. We remember Blake's assertion that "Everything that lives is Holy".

The manuscript bore the subtitle "Breakfast Before Execution" which makes us think of the Last Supper while still making a play on the word "break".

The syllabic structure of the poem, however, is *un*broken, with lines of 8, 8, 4, 8, 8 syllables in each stanza.

l.2 A FOREIGN TREE: both the vine and the cross.

l.10 MAN BROKE THE SUN: with a play on the word Son (Christ).

ll.11–12 Because of the line-ending, we get the notion of sacrificial blood-letting ("this blood you let").

22 When once the twilight locks
(*Notebook* version November 1933; thoroughly revised by March 1934)

Compare Thomas's *A process in the weather of the heart* and *Before I knocked*.

"I'm enclosing one poem just finished. It's quite my usual stuff, I'm afraid …" Thomas's comment on sending the early version of this poem to Pamela Hansford Johnson emphasises how highly characteristic it was of his often morbid concern with the individual's progress from the womb towards death, though mitigated here by the final stanza's healthy commitment to ordinary life. The poem also dramatizes fears and hopes regarding his career *as poet*.

First two stanzas: with the foetus and the amniotic fluid no longer "locked in" by the "twilight locks" of the womb, and with the period of suckling over ("When the galactic sea was sucked"), the physical "creature" (described as if by his alter ego, his own more intellectual consciousness) is sent "scouting on the globe" of an equally creaturely world.

Stanza Three laments that this mortal "creature" only briefly celebrates the world of light ("held a little sabbath with the sun"), surrendering instead to the world of night and dreams ("He drowned his father's magics in a dream").

Stanzas Four–Six are as if an evocation of those dreams – the obsessive morbid fantasies of adolescence perhaps, but also possibly literal night-mares or the often grotesque imaginative world of Thomas's own early poems – replete with images expressing a pained fascination with disease and death.

Stanza Seven recapitulates the birth processes of the two opening stanzas. In the *final stanza* the speaker exhorts his other self to awake from his morbid dreaming to the reality of ordinary day-to-day creative living, where worlds of opportunity and promise "hang on the trees".

l.3 DAMMED: an image of the womb as a river-lock or dam. The likelihood also of a pun on 'damned' is suggested by Thomas's comment in a letter to Vernon Watkins – "locked in these damned days".

ll.9–19 The sequence "scouting" ... "flask" ... "fuses timed" ... "charge" ... "powder" ... "all issue armoured" suggests old-fashioned firearms.

l.17 DREW ... THE STRAWS OF SLEEP: this submerged image of drawing lots (in a gamble) is confirmed later in l.34: "By trick or *chance* he fell asleep".

l.24 CHRIST-CROSS-ROW = the alphabet. (A cross was placed before a row of letters in early spelling-books.)

l.26 SARGASSO: the Sargasso Sea (in the North Atlantic) is comprised of floating seaweed with berry-like air-vessels.

l.45 PICKTHANK: archaic and dialect word for 'sycophant' and 'tell-tale', found in Shakespeare, Blake and Joyce. "Poppied" here means 'drugged' (with sleep).

23 Where once the waters of your face
(*Notebook* version March 1934)

Compare Wordsworth's *Ode: Intimations of Immortality*, and Thomas's *Poem in October* and *Fern Hill*.
In a letter roughly contemporary with this poem, Thomas wrote to Trevor Hughes: "This new year has brought back to my mind the sense of magic that was lost – irretrievably I thought – so long ago." In the poem, Thomas uses the image of a rich and magical sea to denote a sense of wonder and optimism which he feels has passed, and the image of a dry sea bed to suggest the death of his childlike intuitions. As Wordsworth put it, "Shades of the prison-house begin to close/Upon the growing Boy".
Each stanza has the same syllable count – 8, 8, 6, 8, 8, 6.

l.1 WATERS OF YOUR FACE: cf. Genesis i. 2 – "And the Spirit of God moved upon the face of the waters."

l.2 SPUN TO MY SCREWS: an abstract paraphrase might be 'Did my bidding'. The image also wittily suggests a boat's propellers. But it seems possible that a more private meaning also exists: in another poem, Thomas has the phrase "the screws that turn the voice", so he might be implying that the sea responded to his poetic voice. Cf. "sang to my horn" in *Fern Hill*.

l.13 INVISIBLE: though the sea has withdrawn, the poet's imagination keeps it present as a potential.

ll.16–17 THE SHADES/OF CHILDREN: a crucial phrase which suggests that the subject of the poem is the child's growth to maturity (cf. "the childless land" of *Fern Hill*). That part of the poet which is still childlike continues to yearn for the rich world of the imagination ("the dolphined sea", l.18).

ll.19–24 The final stanza affirms that the poet will strive to regain the child's vision. With "serpents" (l.23) Thomas was probably evoking something like the Loch Ness monster, which he refers to in the letter quoted above, claiming also that "I am conscious, if not of the probability of the impossible, at least of its possibility". But of course "serpents" also acknowledges the presence of corruption inside all Edens.

24 Our eunuch dreams (*Notebook* version March 1934)

Compare C. Day Lewis's *Newsreel* and Thomas's *When once the twilight locks*.

"There is no reason at all why I should not write of gunmen, cinemas & pylons if what I have to say necessitates it" (Thomas to Pamela Hansford Johnson). The poem is nevertheless more 'contemporary' in its subject-matter than is usual for Thomas, concerned as it is with the unreal fictions of cinema as well as with the barren ("eunuch") dreams of adolescence. Like the dreams of '*When once the twilight locks*', the fictions of the cinema deprive the individual of his "faith" (ll.29 and 36) in the world of actuality.

l.2 OF LIGHT AND LOVE: the syntax is 'Our eunuch dreams ... of light and love'.

l.5 GROOMS: a verb, a truncated form of '[Bride] grooms' – ie. the dreams become the husbands of "the dark brides".

l.26 WELSHING RICH: to 'welsh' is to fail to honour a debt in gambling. A characteristic dig also at the stuffiness ("starch") and hypocrisy of the pillars of society of his bourgeois Swansea upbringing.

25 I see the boys of summer (*Notebook* version April 1934)

Compare Thomas Hardy's *To an Unborn Pauper Child*.

The poet accuses the "boys of summer" of suppressing their natural sexuality. These "boys" can be taken to be the people he sees around him in his immediate community, and in stanzas three and four they are the unborn children who will become tomorrow's adolescents and adults. Most critics argue that Section II is spoken by the "boys of summer" themselves, in reply, and that Section III is a line-by-line dialogue between them and Thomas. The present editor believes that the whole poem is just as easily spoken by the poet on his own.

Only line 47 breaks a syllable count of 11, 7, 10, 8, 8, 10 in each stanza.

The following stanza-by-stanza guide is designed to suggest the 'argument' of the poem, and therefore does not gloss all individual phrases and images. The main aspect the reader should note is the way in which the images constantly suggest the opposites, sexuality–frigidity, growth–decay, life–death. See also the discussion of the poem in the Introduction. *Stanza One*: The boys of summer deny sexual fruition; they freeze, instead of using, their sexual potency. *Stanza Two*: They allow that which is sweet and productive to turn sour; masturbation takes the place of intercourse; they live off moral notions of "doubt and dark"; the female principle ("signal moon") means nothing to them. *Stanzas Three and Four*: The poet imagines the unborn children, and thinks they will grow ("stature") into "men of nothing" who will avoid sexual "heats"; their hearts already pump the warm pulse of conventional morality ("love and light"); but the natural pulse of blood is frozen, though seen as a potential by the poet.

Stanza Five: But, however the poet may despair, birth must happen – or *real* death takes over. *Stanza Six*: The poet now cynically acts as the spokesman of "the dark deniers", the society responsible for this frigid morality, summoning from the womb death instead of life, and scarecrows instead of vital flesh-and-blood. *Stanza Seven*: Speaking now as one of the "summer boys" already born, he attends at the birth of future generations, celebrated not with a bouquet, but with a cynically offered wreath.

Stanza Eight: He claims that society as good as crucifies sexuality ("merry squires" = sexual organs); the sexual organ "dries and dies"; a kiss is allowed, but in the quarry of "no love". The last line, however, again points to the phallic "poles of promise" in the newly born.

Stanza Nine: A recapitulation. The final line suggests that their birth may change things. The image in that line is of the poles of two circles (womb and world) touching, as they merge into one at the moment of birth.

26 If I were tickled by the rub of love
(*Notebook* version April 1934)

Compare Thomas's *Before I knocked*.

In the first four stanzas the poet imagines, respectively, four stages of life – unborn embryo, baby, adolescent, and old man. If he were "tickled" (either physically or in the sense of being 'amused') by the "rub" (again, either physical or in Hamlet's sense of 'obstacle') of any of the experiences associated with those stages of life, he would not fear abstract philosophies, historic events, or death. Instead, "the only rub that tickles" – that moves him as man and poet – is a morbid fascination with mortality: "I sit and watch the worm beneath my nail/Wearing the quick away". As with Hamlet, this diseased obsession has unfortunately become the very essence of his sensibility. The poem ends with a prayer that full, living, objective mankind become his subject-matter: "Man be my metaphor".

l.2 ROOKING: thieving and exorbitant.

ll.6–7 APPLE ... FLOOD: of Adam and Noah.

l.11 WINGING BONE: as with the classical god, Hermes.

ll.23–28 Several words here have been isolated from familiar pairs – *butter ... flies, lock ... jaws, sea ... Dead* (Dead Sea).

l.33 HERRINGS SMELLING: in the sense 'searching for' as well as 'smelly' (herrings are scavenging fish).

27 Especially when the October wind (October 1934)

Two major themes come together in this poem. First, stemming from the fact that October was Thomas's birth month, there are the intimations of decay traditionally associated with autumn. The other, confirmed by similar statements in the letters and by an earlier, more prosaic version of the poem, is the theme of what we might call the tyranny of words, but which philosophers call the problem of 'nominalism and universals'. For Thomas, word and thing seem indivisible: "When I experience anything, I experience it as a thing and a word at the same time, both equally amazing" (quoted by Alastair Reid).

Thomas seems to have worked to a basic count of 10 syllables per line.
Stanza One: The ordinary sensations of an October day, forecasting dissolution, makes his heart 'shudder' and respond in words, in poetry.
Stanza Two: The "tower of words" is both the poet's body and the house in which he works. The reality of the women is for him literary ("wordy"), and the children in the park opposite cause him to make a pun on "rows" and fix on the star-pattern made by their arms and legs. He would like to communicate the reality of the "beeches" etc. at a level deeper than that of language; but the 'vowels', "voices" "notes" and "speeches" of words are his only tools. l.10 WALKING LIKE THE TREES: the blind man healed by Christ (Mark, viii. 24) said "I see men as trees walking". An earlier version of Thomas's line had been "Men in the distance walk like trees".
Stanza Three: Things are communicated to him, not through words, but at the level of nervous ("neural") response. If only he could "tell" us what the meadow or the raven signifies in as wordless a way as the clock or grass "tells" him about the passing of time.
Stanza Four: But the poet gives in to the necessary limitations of words (though, within the brackets, he still emphasizes the wordless communications of nature). He now accepts his dependence on "heartless words" – heartless because they have been "drained" from the heart, and because they are not themselves alive. But having made these "heartless words" (having, that is, written this poem), his heart is now suitably word-less; and the final line asks us to listen, not to the words of this poem, but to the message of the "dark-vowelled birds".

28 Should lanterns shine (November 1934)

Compare *Why east wind chills*.
The theme is the young man's determination to remain open to experience instead of seeking 'answers' or 'solutions' to the mystery of life. Something Keats once said is a good thing to bear in mind on approaching the poem – the need to allow "only a gradual ripening of the intellectual powers".
ll.1–8 The whole first stanza is a metaphor for man's tendency to probe

and pry into the unknown. The image is of breaking into an Egyptian-style burial chamber, and finding the mummy disintegrating even as one looks at it.

l.2 OCTAGON: probably because the aperture of the lantern is octagonal, or because the tomb itself is.

ll.3–4 AND ANY BOY ... FROM GRACE: any boy born of love, or intending love. There is a suggestion of necrophilia.

l.6 FALSE DAY: because *a* the lantern's light is artificial light, and *b* this is only a parody of the real Judgment Day.

ll.9–15 HEART ... HEAD ... PULSE: Three 'philosophies of life' which the young man has had urged upon him. He mistrusts each one in isolation. "like head" (l.10) refers back to the first stanza, which was an image of the workings of pure reason.

ll.11–14 cf. Andrew Marvell's *To His Coy Mistress*:

> Rather at once our Time devour,
> Than languish in his slow-chapt pow'r.
> . . . .
> Thus, though we cannot make our Sun
> Stand still, yet we will make him run.

l.17 SOME CHANGE: either change as the result of the advice ("telling"), or change in the advice itself.

ll.18–19 The "ball" is an image of a question, to which no answer has "yet reached the ground". Time and experience have to be lived through before they become, in themselves, the answer. The image is one of many memories in the poetry of Cwmdonkin Park, near Thomas's childhood home in Swansea.

29 and 30 'Altarwise' Sonnets I and IV
(Sonnet I – February 1935; Sonnet IV – September 1935)

Compare John Donne's 'Holy Sonnets' and 'La Corona' sonnets.
Arguably the most difficult of his poems, the ten 'Altarwise' sonnets strenuously combine the poet's autobiography with that of Christ, the sexual with the religious, and the flippant or sacrilegious with the proud and momentous. From the 'nativity' of Sonnet I to the 'resurrection' and 'gospel' aftermath of Sonnets IX and X, the sequence includes several aspects of the Christian story – the preaching, the fasting, the crucifixion – but is highly heterodox in its treatment of them. A major difficulty, beyond understanding the syntax or being able to visualize the images, is that of gauging the tone intended.
SONNET I. Christ's God-ordained crucifixion is seen as defeating Death and as involving also the castration of Christ's physical, sexual attributes. Then, *as if contemporaneously*, this dead Christ appears at the cradle of the newly-born poet (or at the manger of the newly-born Christ-child himself).

A PARAPHRASED NARRATIVE WOULD RUN AS FOLLOWS:

ll.1 – 6: *Lying horizontally* ("altarwise") *in a dim light* ("owl-light") *in the* "half-way house" *of the tomb, Christ* ("the gentleman") *and his human passions and appetites* ("his furies") *lay as a captive of the grave* ("graveward"); *the Angel of Death ("Abaddon"), inherent in human flesh* ("hangnail") *but pinned at the crucifixion* ("hangnail"), *split away from* ("cracked from") *Adam. From Christ's groin* ("fork"), *God* (a "dog among the fairies" of lesser gods, and an "atlas-eater with a jaw for news" – world-devouring and able to taste future events) *bit out Christ's sexual organs, man-shaped and as if uttering the scream of future progeny* ("Bit out the mandrake with tomorrow's scream").

ll.7 – 14: *Then, with eyes cold and dead like pennies* (also "penny-eyed" because pennies used to be placed on the eyes of the dead), *Christ* ("that gentleman of wounds"), *born out of nothing or out of heaven* ("Old cock from nowheres and the heaven's egg"), *with his* "bones unbuttoned to the half-way winds" *of either the tomb or his existence between life and death, and resurrected* ("hatched") *from the storm-struck detritus of the cross* ("the windy salvage on one leg"), "scraped at my cradle in a walking word" *that time of night and that period in Time* ("that night of time") *under the* "Christward shelter" *– at once, both the poet's birthplace and Christ's Bethlehem.* "I am the long world's gentleman, he said,/ And share my bed with Capricorn and Cancer" *– spanning the geographic scope of the whole world (its tropics) and also embodying both its lustful energy* ("Capricorn" – the Goat) *and its diseased death* ("Cancer").

l.3 ABADDON: the angel of the bottomless pit (Revelation ix.11).

l.6 MANDRAKE: Mandragora, whose man-shaped root was ascribed powers of fertility (Genesis xxx. 14–16). Reputed to utter a scream and cause fatal effects when uprooted – so a dog was used in the uprooting (hence the sonnet's canine images).

SONNET IV. Line 6, an 'aside' within brackets – "(Questions are hunchbacks to the poker marrow)" – claims that the questions which form the bulk of the sonnet's opening are lame and deformed ones that cannot have answers and that represent the futile probings of man's presumptuous intellect. (Compare the similar questions in *Why east wind chills*.) The speaker, in the persona of a growing boy, is as if asking these questions of the crucified Christ who appeared to him – "(My shape of age nagging the wounded whisper)". Christ replies, not only with his ability to pierce through all vain outward shows to the skeleton beneath (ll.9–10), but with an impressive image of love. Love is like recognizing some faces as ones you saw projected on the wall of the womb before you were born. But "mushroom features" – suggesting the vagueness of a face seen in extreme "close-up" – also vividly suggests the face of the embryo itself, so that the "love" can be, conversely, an adult's love of the person that that imagined embryo will become. That this is the meaning of the sonnet's cinematographic last four lines is shown by an explanation that Dylan Thomas wrote in the poem's margin in Edith Sitwell's copy of *Twenty-five Poems* (now at the Humanities Research Centre, the University of Texas): "Love is a reflection of the features (the features of those you will know and love *after* the womb) which are photographed before birth on the wall of the womb." As it continues, the note speaks of "the womb being surrounded by food; a field being its own field, and the womb being its own food."

31 Incarnate devil (*Notebook* version May 1933, much revised and shortened for publication in August 1935)

Like Blake, Thomas here sees the separation of good and evil as a case of abstract distinctions, superimposed upon man's deeper instincts. Compare Blake in *The Marriage of Heaven and Hell*: "Without contraries is no progression. Attraction and Repulsion, Reason and Energy, Love and Hate, are necessary to Human existence. From these contraries spring what the religious call Good & Evil. Good is the passive that obeys Reason. Evil is the active springing from Energy."

The following is a working paraphrase, which by no means follows through every suggestion made by the poem's images:

Stanza One: The Biblical Eden, seen in a way which makes God guilty of setting an arbitrary trap for man. Through the serpent (which the poet would rather see as the vitality which "stung awake" the "circle" of the apple, the garden, or the world itself), God gave the *appearance* of evil ("shapes of sin") to the "forked" Tree of Knowledge. He prohibited ("forked out") and set apart ("forked out") the apple which "bearded" God Himself had created. In this event, God acted the part of unconcerned "fiddling" Nero and deceitful ("fiddling") boss – having in the first place arranged it to exercise His own power of pardon, and minimizing ('playing down') His own need for pardon in such trickery.

Stanza Two: Scholars tell me that in pagan times, when men were strangers to the idea of God-controlled seas or the idea that God created the moon by hand, the pagan deities *united* good and evil. The moon, itself a deity, was black *and* white in its significance for man, not the one-sided white ("half holy", 'half whole') of Christian thought.

Stanza Three: In our own non-mythological Eden (in the womb or in childhood), we had an intuitive ("secret") belief in a force ("guardian". Innocence?) which would keep that paradise from the Fall of Experience. But the notion of a burning Hell, or the idea that things are either good or bad ("the cloven myth"), or that the only heaven comes through the death of Christ ('midnight of the Son') which occurred in darkness ("midnight of the sun") – these were the "fiddled" tunes and "fiddled" tricks of a Christian God, seen now as the serpent itself.

32 O make me a mask
(*Notebook* version March 1933, rephrased and severely shortened
November 1937)

Compare Thomas's *I have longed to move away*, *Ears in the turrets hear*,
and *To Others than You*.

The poem's speaker seeks defence of inner privacy against the sharp
examination of outsiders or critics.

Except for line 7, all the lines have 13 syllables.

l.2 ENAMELLED EYES ... SPECTACLED CLAWS: the adjectives have been
   interchanged. For "spectacled claws", cf. Milton's phrase in *Paradise
   Lost*, "sagacious of his quarry from afar".

l.3 Behind a face of innocence, he seeks to hide the harrowing effects of
   time and experience.

l.4 BARE ENEMIES: "bare" because they would be disarmed by his pretence.

l.10 BELLADONNA: Deadly Nightshade. The literal meaning (Beautiful
   Lady) contrasts with the pretended modesty of "widower grief".

ll.10–12 From behind his own pretence, he will more easily detect the
   pretence of others. The "curve of the nude mouth" and "the laugh up
   the sleeve" belong to the speaker and his enemies alike.

33 How shall my animal (March 1938)

Compare Thomas's *My hero bares his nerves* and *The force that through
the green fuse*.

"I hold a beast, an angel and a madman in me, and my enquiry is as to
their working, and my problem is their subjugation and victory, down-
throw & upheaval, and my effort is their self-expression. The new poem
I enclose, 'How Shall My Animal', is a detailed enquiry; and the poem
too is the result of the enquiry ... The poem is, as all poems are, its own
question and answer, its own contradiction, its own agreement. I ask only
that my poetry should be taken literally" (Thomas to Henry Treece). The
full force of this poem's account of dragging up a weird monster from a
deep internal lair is certainly dependent on our surrendering to its
concreteness rather than reducing it to paraphrase. Nevertheless, it seems
clear that the "animal" is some kind of metaphor for dark inner material
that risks being killed in being transformed into language (made to
"endure burial under the *spelling* wall" of the poem or of the poet's
mouth). Relevant to what is in many ways a Lawrentian poem, is what
Lawrence says in *Psychoanalysis and the Unconscious*: "'In the beginning
was the Word'. This is the presumptuous masquerading of the mind. The
word cannot be the beginning of life". The poet's fears are of the death,
in language, of the "animal" – the great elemental forces – within him.

l.14 LIONHEAD: cf. Revelation ix. 9 – "The heads of the horses were like
   lion's heads". The word was suggested by Vernon Watkins.

ll.34–36 The sequence "shorn" ... "sly scissors" ... "thicket of strength"
   ... "pillars" evokes the story of the Biblical Samson.

34 When all my five and country senses (March 1938)

The speaker of this sonnet is an unborn human being. He looks forward to two distinct stages after birth: *a* ll.1–12, the stage of an ordinary life-span and *b* ll.13–14, the stage after death. Stage *a* is when our understanding is informed by (and restricted to) our physical senses. Stage *b* is the different situation after death when there is a kind of organic, cosmic consciousness – undivided, and no longer open to disappointment.

Only line 13 breaks a regular count of 10 syllables per line.

ll.1–10 Four senses (touch, hearing, taste, smell) are described as having the power of 'seeing', which is of course the fifth sense. What they will 'see' in life is how love is all the time being reduced, delayed, driven out and ruined.

l.1 COUNTRY: 'physical', also suggesting that each sense is a separate "country" (cf. "love's countries", l.12).

ll.3–4 The 'halfmoons' on the fingernails are compared also to the "husk of young stars". Like Zodiacal signs on a human hand, they forecast the death and denial of "love".

l.8 LASHED TO SYLLABLES: 'whipped to pieces' and/or 'tied (limited) to words'. The tongue will be powerless to remedy the injury done to love.

ll.9, 10 HER: love's.

l.14 After death, the heart will continue a "sensual", sub-intellectual consciousness as part of the organic world itself.

35 After the funeral (In memory of Ann Jones) (March–April 1938)

Compare Hopkins's *Felix Randal*, and the first story in Thomas's *Portrait of the Artist as a Young Dog*.

Ann Jones was the poet's maternal aunt who lived at Fern Hill, where Thomas spent many schoolboy holidays. After the hypocrisy of the mourners (ll.1–5) and the emotional poverty of the poet's first response to Ann's death (ll.7–8), Thomas offers an exaggerated 'Bardic' eulogy which is made to contrast with the old woman's simplicity (ll.16–20) and with the pious finality of her death (ll.31–35). A sustained theme is the inadequacy of language to keep human reality alive; but the poem's poignancy lies nevertheless in that attempt.

ll.1–12 The first word "After" governs the whole of lines 1–11; the first main verb is "I stand" (l.12).

l.5 SPITTLED EYES: the mourner's eyes show only a pretence at grief.

ll.6–8 In the presence (presumably) of the open coffin in the farm parlour early on the morning of the funeral, the young boy was at the time incapable of adequate emotion, shedding "dry leaves" instead of tears; but a promise was made that he would produce the "dry leaves" of a future poem.

l.25 A BROWN CHAPEL: the natural chapel of "the ferned and foxy woods".

l.27 THIS SKYWARD STATUE: the exaggerated description of Ann is compared to a monumental statue on a gravestone.

l.37 GESTURE AND PSALM: as nouns, the "gesture" made by Ann's imagined statue and the "psalm" of the poem's praise; as also verbs, the two words are in apposition to "storm" in the next line.

ll.36–40 The sense of these last five lines is a hope that the exaggerated description of Ann and the poem itself will keep alive the poet's emotional relationship to the old woman, and return a less artificial life to the home and community she has left.

ll.39–40 The imagery here derives from a favourite book, Djuna Barnes's *Nightwood*: "if one gave birth to a heart on a plate, it would say 'Love,' and twitch like the lopped leg of a frog".

36 The tombstone told (September 1938)

Compare Philip Larkin's *Deceptions*.

Thomas, in a letter, described this poem as "Hardy-like", referring presumably to its anecdotal quality. From several time-angles, the poem converges on the fate of a girl who died before the sexual fulfilment of her marriage-night.

l.2 HER TWO SURNAMES: her maiden and her married surnames.

ll.6–9 Her marriage occurred before the poet was conceived. But the embryo's pre-natal experience of life and death was as good as being a *fore*casting vision of this girl's individual dead body.

ll.11–20 (Second Stanza). After coming across her grave, the poet hears gossip of how she had died. Dying itself was like the sexual fulfilment which was in actuality denied her (ll.17–20).

l.11 A STRANGER: her husband – whom Death prevented her getting to know, or 'knowing' sexually.

ll.13–15. This happened (the poet repeats) before the poet's pre-natal vision of the girl's dead body, before the rain running through her heart "spoke" (l.8) her death to the embryo in the womb ('the room of a secret child').

l.21 I WHO SAW is the embryo who experienced her death like a film thrown on the "mortal wall" of the womb.

l.24 HEARD refers to the poet's experience while actually standing by her grave. Now, as if speaking through the "stone bird" carved on her tombstone, the girl describes her own death.

ll.29–30 These two final lines concentrate two ideas: the sexual fulfilment of death, and the *imagined* birth of a son.

37 On no work of words (September 1938)

Compare Milton's sonnet "When I consider how my light is spent",
Keats's sonnet "When I have fears that I may cease to be", and Hopkins's
sonnet *To R[obert] B[ridges]*.

To partake of the created world involves, for the artist, the responsibility
of reproducing its creativity in return. From the word "rich" (l.2) springs
a sustained series of financial imagery.

l.1 The line suggests being on the dole.

l.3 TAKE TO TASK: reprimand; but also, literally, 'bring to the job' which
needs doing.

l.4 HUNGRILY: God sent down manna to feed the hungry Israelites
(Exodus xvi), some of whom refused the gift so that the manna "bred
worms and stank". The position of "hungrily" here suggests that God
himself is hungry for a response.

l.5 cf. George Herbert's images for *Prayer*: "reversed thunder", "exalted
manna".

l.6 Unused, the poet's "gift" for words returns as an insult ("bangs
back"), its powers of revelation wasted ("blind").

l.7 TO LIFT TO LEAVE: to accept and then abandon is a form of stealing
('lifting').

 TREASURES OF MAN: either the wonders of the created world, or the
poems of other poets (?).

ll.8–9 Death will, like a cashier, balance all used opportunities against
those left unused, in a final judgment.

l.10 OGRE: Death.

 TWICE: Death takes, not only the poet's body, but also that body of
poetry he failed to produce.

ll.11–12 In a sense, the world exists only as we, in responding to it, are
constantly recreating it ("this world … is each man's work", l.12).
Thus if the poet merely exhausts it selfishly ("burn", l.12), it dwindles
(the forest becomes the nut again). If, however, he under*takes* to
respond creatively, the creation of the world will be reproduced in each
poem (the nut will be seen to produce the woods again).

l.11 THE NUT OF THE SEAS: all life is thought to have originated in the sea.
'The oaktree came out of the acorn; the woods of my blood came out
of the nut of the sea, the tide-concealing, blood-red kernel' (letter to
Desmond Hawkins).

l.12 WHICH IS EACH MAN'S WORK: with "to return" as its subject, this clause
reads 'which is each man's duty'; with "world" as its subject, it reads
'which is each man's creation'.

38 Twenty-four years (October 1938)

Written a few days before the poet's twenty-fourth birthday. Compare
Milton's sonnet on *his* twenty-fourth birthday, "How soon hath Time,
the subtle thief of youth".

l.2 IN LABOUR: with difficulty; but also in the act of giving birth. The line,
one supposes, is mainly relevant because of its ominous tone, reminis-
cent of an 'Aside' in a Jacobean tragedy.

l.3 NATURAL DOORWAY: the entrance of the womb, where life's "journey"
starts.

l.4 SHROUD: both the winding-sheet in which the dead body will be finally
dressed, and the flesh of the body itself.

ll.6–8 Life is seen as keeping a date with death ("dressed ... strut ... money
... direction ... town").

l.6 DIE: also a pun on the Elizabethan sense of sexual fulfilment.

l.8 ELEMENTARY: death seen as a primary, basic fact. The word also
suggests 'elemental'.

l.9 The speaker is open-minded as to how long Time is, or whether
Eternity exists. This last line transforms the melodrama of the poem
into a note of resignation, with a subtle suggestion of value ("ad-
vance") and the irony of having a poem about death end with the verb
'to be' – "as long as forever *is*".

39 Once it was the colour of saying (December 1938)

Compare Yeats's *A Coat* and *The Circus Animals' Desertion*, and Robert
Graves's *The Cool Web*.

A kind of interim report on the poet's own career. Thomas feels that
hitherto the glamour of words has counted more with him than the
human experience which poetry ought to be exploring.

l.1 COLOUR OF SAYING: the rhetorical and aesthetic sound and shape of
words, as opposed to what they actually mean. Cf. James Joyce's
Portrait of the Artist as a Young Man: "He drew forth a phrase from
his treasure and spoke it softly to himself: – A day of dappled seaborne
clouds. The phrase and the day and the scene harmonised in a chord.
Words. Was it their colours?"

l.2 SOAKED: the first of several hints that his love for mere language tended
to drown and wash away the reality of his subjects ("soaked ...
capsized ... seaslides ... drowned"). The "table" is his writing-table.

UGLIER SIDE OF A HILL: Thomas's childhood home at Cwmdonkin Drive,
Swansea was on a very steep suburban hill ("uglier" than the country
the other side).

l.3 CAPSIZED: the steep road made the field opposite the house appear as
if on the wrong level. The word also suggests 'the size of a cap'.

ll.5–6 The glamorous language had drowned the people and other realities in the poems. Now they will resurrect themselves ("arise"), herald a new dawn in the poet's career ("cock-crow"), and "kill" the old poet.

l.7 MITCHING: dialect word common in Wales = 'playing truant'.

l.8 CUCKOO: mad, silly.

ll.10–11 "Shade", a word denoting darkness, had been capable of several "shades" (associations) of meaning – and therefore something spectacular and *colour*ful ("a lamp of lightning").

l.12 Now his poetry *a* shall be an "undoing" of his old manner (cf. "I must undo", l.5); *b* shall savour less of the poet himself and more of outside reality; *c* may even be the *final* end of him as a poet if his new manner is not successful.

l.13 The effect of this last line is to contrast the hard reality ("stone") of the new poetry with the verbal *gentle*ness and *charm* (ll.5–6) of the earlier style; and to contrast a new deliberateness ("wind off like a reel") with the old style's hectic "sea*slides* of saying" (l.5). "Reel" suggests both cinema camera and fishing rod.

40 If my head hurt a hair's foot (March 1939)

Compare Thomas Hardy's *To An Unborn Pauper Child*, Louis MacNeice's *Prayer Before Birth*, and Sylvia Plath's *Nick and the Candlestick*.

Thomas's first child, Llewelyn, was born in January 1939. *Stanzas One–Three* are spoken by an unborn child; *stanzas Four–Six* are the mother's reply to the child's fears of causing her pain in birth. "It is not a narrative, nor an argument, but a series of conflicting images which move through pity and violence to an unreconciled acceptance of suffering: the mother's *and* the child's. This poem has been called obscure. I refuse to believe that it is obscurer than pity, violence, or suffering. But being a poem, not a lifetime, it is more compressed" (Thomas in a broadcast).

l.4 WORM OF THE ROPES: the umbilical cord; Thomas made "ropes" plural to suggest its coiled appearance, and also to introduce several images of the boxing-ring.

l.5 BULLY ILL LOVE: the verb is "bully ill".

CLOUTED: in the sense of both 'beaten' and 'cloths'.

l.9 THE GHOST WITH A HAMMER, AIR: Thomas would have known that Jimmy Wilde, the Welsh boxing hero, was nicknamed 'The ghost with a hammer in his hand'.

l.12 THE MAKING HOUSE: the womb.

l.16–17 The mother would not change this birth for the presumably gentler birth of Christ or the slow process which brings mother-of-pearl (nacre) into being.

l.20 One allusion is to the 'breaking of the waters' of the womb, technically the first stage of birth.

l.30 "Prodigies" here suggests that *all* children are marvels. This one birth ("beginning"), though painful ("suffers"), is "endless" and "open" because it will lead to countless others.

41 To Others than You (May 1939)

Compare Thomas's *O make me a mask* and W. H. Davies's *Evil*.
The poet's accusation is that friendship has been used as a cover to lay bare his inner privacy. The main syntax runs: "You ... Whom now I conjure to stand as thief ... Were once such a creature ... (That) I never thought to utter or think ... That ... My friends were enemies on stilts ..."

l.1 BY ENEMY: by calling you an enemy.

l.17 DISPLACED A TRUTH: by speaking a lie.

42 When I woke (July 1939)

Compare Wilfred Owen's *The Promisers* ("When I awoke, the glancing day looked gay").
Morning sounds in Laugharne wake Thomas from his private nightmares and to his work as a poet. But a new "voice" heralds a different nightmare – the outbreak of the Second World War – which will end the ordinary world as he knows it. "This war, trembling even on the edge of Laugharne, fills me with such horror and terror and lassitude" (in a letter to Vernon Watkins).

ll.3–7 The images are from the world of his own nightmares. "Dispelled" (l.6) = not only 'dispersed' but 'broke the spell of'.

ll.8–15 An ordinary workman, concerned only with the physical, 'cuts the morning off' from the world of nightmare, as if he were killing the "last snake" of the poet's dream-world or the "wand or subtle bough" which would lead him back into nightmare.

ll.16–21 The poet sees himself as God (because he creates a world in his poetry), capable of miracle (walking on the water), and marking the "fall" of the "sparrow" and of the "death-stagged scatter-breath mammoth".

l.25 ERECTED AIR: either because the announcement of war comes over the radio, or because the clocks and bells of l.28 are on 'erected' towers.

ll.29–30 The two final images of "white sheet" and "coins on my eyelids" suggest death. There are second meanings to both "islands" ("eyelands") and "shells" (bombs).

43 Paper and sticks (Autumn 1939)

Thomas included this poem in his fourth volume of poetry, *Deaths and*

Entrances (1946), but omitted it from his *Collected Poems* (1952) at the proof stage.

44 There was a saviour (February 1940)

"The churches are wrong, because they standardize our gods, because they label our morals, because they laud the death of a vanished Christ, and fear the crying of the new Christ in the wilderness" (letter to Pamela Hansford Johnson).

The poem emphasizes man's *individual* responsibility for love and compassion. In the past, Christianity has been a kind of comforting other-worldly retreat from that responsibility. Now, in a less religious age, and in the first winter of the Second World War, human tragedy is brought home to each individual conscience. In this direct confrontation with those who have perverted Christ's teaching, Thomas gains an added irony by using the stanza-form of Milton's *On the Morning of Christ's Nativity*, which Kathleen Raine recalls was Thomas's favourite poem.

Stanza One describes those first Christians who thus blinded themselves to outside reality. *Stanza Two* is spoken by those Christians themselves, confessing their fault. *Stanza Three* is addressed by the poet to those Christians, repeating the accusation. *Stanzas Four and Five* are spoken by the poet and one of those nominal Christians, the poet thereby confessing his own guilt in the matter.

l.4 CHILDREN: either the earliest Christian believers or literally children (perhaps in Sunday School?).

l.8 JAILS AND STUDIES: Christianity seen as a teaching and a discipline to which men blindly confine themselves. The word "keyless", however, suggests that the fault lies with Christians, not with Christ. Christ's actual teaching involved, not easy safety, but *'cruel* truth' (l.3), "safe *unrest*" (l.11), *"murdering* breath" (l.14) etc.

l.10 LOST WILDERNESS: the 'safety' of blind Christianity was not a paradise but a "wilderness", divorced from the actual world of men.

ll.22-23 Their emotion was directed to heaven, not to earth.

l.24 Now the responsibility falls directly on individuals.

l.25 BLACKED: morally guilty; caught in the darkness of individual responsibility; but also in the darkness of a wartime black-out.

l.30 NEAR AND FIRE NEIGHBOUR: "fire" evokes the blitz; but there is also a play on 'near and far'.

l.32 LITTLE KNOWN FALL: the death of any ordinary person, as opposed to the more 'famous' fall of Adam or the death of Christ.

ll.37-38 The dust of dead strangers enters through doors previously closed to them.

ll.39-40 The love which had previously been isolated inside each individual. The "rocks" it will 'break' could be the rock of cruelty, the rock guarding Christ's tomb, and even the rock of the church itself.

45 Deaths and Entrances (summer 1940)

Compare Thomas's *There was a saviour* and *Among those Killed in the Dawn Raid was a Man Aged a Hundred*.

The poet called this his "poem about invasion", and it was written after a particular air raid on London in the summer of 1940 had had a profound effect on him – "I get nightmares like invasions". The "you" addressed throughout is any person on the 'eve' of actual death in such "incendiary" raids. A phrase in the third and last stanza – the "near and strange" casualties of the London raids – helps with the referents of the first two stanzas. "Near" relates to friends and loved ones, a representative of whom is described in the first stanza as falling into the silence of endless mourning at "your" death; and "strange" relates to one of those who are not actually known to you ("sun [son] of another street") but who are on your side in the war (an R.A.F. fighter pilot seems intended) and will sacrifice himself in your defence. But one figure above all will detect and reach you – Death itself, seen in the close-up image of a German airman crashing in the very act of killing you (the letter quoted above describes a "'plane brought down in Tottenham Court Road").

DEATHS AND ENTRANCES(title): from John Donne's sermon *Death's Duell* – "Deliverance from that death, the death of the wombe, is an entrance, a delivery over to another death".

l.12 MARRIED LONDON: the adjective suggests family life. Cf. Philip Larkin's "married villages" (*How Distant*).

l.33 DARKENED KEYS: apart from "keys" that open locks, another association for this image is suggested in the letter quoted above about the air raid: "I went to see a smashed aerodrome. Only one person had been killed. He was playing the piano in an entirely empty, entirely dark canteen".

l.36 SAMSON: the destroyer killed in destroying others. Samson also figures in Donne's *Death's Duell* sermon: "Stil pray wee for a peaceable life against violent death ... but never make ill conclusions upon persons overtaken with such deaths ... [God] received Sampson, who went out of this world in such a manner".

46 On the Marriage of a Virgin (January 1941)

Compare Philip Larkin's *Wedding-Wind*.

A working paraphrase of *Stanza One*: When the girl was a virgin, each new morning's sun discovered ("surprised") yesterday's sun asleep (like another guilty lover) on the iris of her now open eye – as if having slept with her. And each new sun was almost like a son born from the previous night's union, leaping "up the sky out of her thighs". Though literally unmarried ("alone"), the virginity which woke up each day in such "a multitude of loves" was, therefore, a "miraculous" one, having produced something like Mary's immaculate conception of Christ, and as old as

Christ himself. But, as the *multiplication* of the loaves and fishes implies, miracles are not unproductive; each miracle is "unending" in what it produces, because each survives the "moment" in which it took place. Thus the "footprints" which Christ made while walking on the waters of Galilee were as productive as a whole "navy of doves" – those birds sacred to Venus and profane love.

l.14 This final line suggests that her new relationship with a single husband is both narrower ("jealous") and greater ("unrivalled").

47 Ballad of the Long-legged Bait (January–April 1941)

Compare John Donne's *The Bait* and Thomas's *Lament*.
The nature of the poem's allegory was several times commented on by Thomas: "a poem about a man who fished with a woman for bait and caught a horrible collection" (to John Davenport); "A young man goes out to fish for sexual experience, but he catches a family, the church, and the village green" (to William York Tindall). On one of the 150 worksheets (now at the University of Buffalo) the poet wrote "Dylan & Caitlin". In his notes about Thomas, Vernon Watkins wrote that "It was so much a visual poem that he made a coloured picture for it which he pinned on the wall of his room, a picture of a woman lying at the bottom of the sea. She was a new Loreley revealing the pitfalls of destruction awaiting those who attempted to put off the flesh". A specific influence on the poem was Rimbaud's *Bateau ivre* ("The Drunken Boat"), which Thomas could have read in Norman Cameron's translation in *New Verse* (June–July 1936), and a more general influence would have been Coleridge's *The Ancient Mariner*.

l. 54 JERICHO ... LUNGS: it was the shouting of the Israelites that brought down the walls of the city (Joshua vi. 20).

l. 68 BULLS OF BISCAY: bull-whales etc. in the Bay of Biscay.

ll. 107–9 SUSANNA ... SHEBA: Susanna, bathing, was lewdly spied upon by two bearded elders (Old Testament Apocrypha). Sheba, visiting Solomon (I Kings x, 1–13), was given "all her desire, whatever she asked", but the only "kings" attending her now are "hungry" ones – the sea's predators.

l. 159 WALKED ON THE EARTH IN THE EVENING: after the Fall, Adam and Eve "heard the voice of the Lord God walking in the garden in the cool of the day" (Genesis iii. 8).

48 Love in the Asylum (April 1941)

Compare Thomas's *On a Wedding Anniversary*.
As with the contemporary 'On a Wedding Anniversary', this poem possibly fictionalizes certain aspects of his still relatively new married status. ('Mad' was a word the poet often teasingly used of himself and

Caitlin.) But perhaps the madness of war is also a background here, and more particularly the contrast of Caitlin's congenial bohemian exuberance with their straitened wartime existence at this period. Homeless, awkwardly squeezed in with his parents in Wales while Caitlin's mother looked after their young son in England, they were desperately looking for rentable rooms elsewhere.

l.8 AT LARGE AS THE DEAD: cf. 'as large as life'.

l.16 TAKEN BY LIGHT IN HER ARMS: the phrase enfolds two different ideas – "taken by light" (sexually possessed by light) and "light in her arms".

49 The hunchback in the park (July 1941)

Compare W. H. Auden's "It was Easter as I walked in the public gardens".

This is not in the ordinary sense fiction: the hunchback, the warning bell, the chained cup etc. were for the poet actual memories of Cwmdonkin Park, Swansea. The relationship of the hunchback to the "figure without fault" (l.32) which he creates is perhaps a suggestion of that between the mortal poet and the created poem; so that Thomas here is, all at once, the narrating poet, one of the tormenting boys, and the hunchback himself.

l.4 LOCK: literally a lock on the park gate, and metaphorically an image of the gate itself as a canal 'lock' allowing entrance and exit.

l.5 The child imagined that the park existed only when he was there. Cf. *Fern Hill*, ll.23–29.

l.31 MADE: possibly the figure is to be thought of as being traced in the dust; but more likely as a daydream of the hunchback's – in a broadcast Thomas spoke of "the bushy Red-Indian-hiding park, where the hunchback sat alone, images of perfection in his head".

50 Among those Killed in the Dawn Raid was a Man Aged a Hundred (July 1941)

Compare Thomas's *A Refusal to Mourn the Death, by Fire, of a Child in London* and *Deaths and Entrances*.

Characteristically, this sonnet refuses to let the *natural* triumph of the old man's death be obscured by piety, officialdom or propaganda. The odd formality of the title comes from the fact that it was an actual headline in a newspaper. (Thomas at one stage considered, as a title for the second part of *Ceremony After a Fire Raid*, 'Among Those Burned to Death Was A Child Aged A Few Hours'.)

l.2 HE DIED: by using this phrase instead of 'was killed', Thomas emphasizes a natural process instead of a political catastrophe. A man aged a hundred is presumably already near death.

l.3 THE LOCKS: in line 11 the man's body is described as a "cage". The "locks" which kept his life in were already 'yawning loose' before the bomb blast "blew them wide".

l.4 LOVED: play on "lived".

l.6 HE STOPPED A SUN: "sun" = bomb. But also literally: for him the sun went out.

ll.10-14 Presumably the ambulance is called "heavenly" because it would be a Red Cross vehicle, collecting the dead for a Christian burial. It is a "common cart" because it collects *all* the dead. The uniqueness of this centenarian victim should give him the right to lie "where he loved". Instead of an ordinary Christian resurrection, the poet stresses that the literal morning is not stopped but quickened by the man's death; and implies that every one of his hundred years will be resurrected by the next hundred births ("storks") in this very place.

51 Lie still, sleep becalmed (April 1944)

This sonnet probably derived its theme from sympathy with the suffering and the dying in wartime. In a more individual connection, however, it would seem to carry memories of the poet's father's suffering from mouth cancer ten years previously.

52 Ceremony After a Fire Raid (May 1944)

"It really is a Ceremony, and the third part of the poem is the music at the end" (Thomas, in a letter).

l.4 AMONG makes the singular "street" stand for *all* streets, as the poet stands for all "grievers".

l.8 DUG: strictly a verb, but also a noun in apposition to "breast".

ll.14-15 The falling "star" of the incendiary bomb (unlike the star which signalled Christ's birth) has ended the "centuries" of human lives which would have come from this one child.

l.21 A GREAT FLOOD: perhaps of the words in this tumultuous poem, metaphorically resuscitating the blood-flow of the dead child.

l.28 BEYOND COCKCROW: beyond actual resurrection.

l.29 THE FLYING SEA: an image for the resurgence of Life.

l.31 LOVE: the creative principle of Life – the first, last, and only fact. The word "spoken" reminds us that "God *said*, Let there be light" and that "In the beginning was the *Word*".

ll.31-32 The poet's only lament at this stage is for the unborn "sons" of the dead child.

ll.33-46 All sacrificed victims are one; this child represents them all; its skeleton is the gravestone (l.44) of all sacrificed innocence.

ll.51-56 The "one child" is mainly Christ who both conquered the serpent and was Himself the "fruit" and 'son' of what the serpent did to Eve.

ll.58–60 Thomas leaves Section II on a note of desolation (as if creation, in this event, had returned to chaos and wilderness), but does so in order to contrast and set off the affirmation of the final section which follows.

li.61–77 The language evokes a literal landscape of burning cathedrals and churches. The surging image of the sea suggests, however, that what will survive is not a Christian consolation as such, but the irresistible, sexual force of life. The "infant-bearing sea" is endless; the fact of birth ("genesis"), once established, is final and "ultimate".

53 and 54 Last night I dived my beggar arm and **Poem** ('Your breath was shed ...') (June 1944)

55 Poem in October (August 1944)

Compare Henry Vaughan's *Regeneration*.
One of the poet's many birthday poems. The location is Laugharne in Carmarthenshire, viewed (from stanza three onwards) from Sir John's Hill. In a letter, Thomas called it "a Laugharne poem: the first place poem I've written".
    Only lines 55 and 56 break the regular syllabic count of 9, 12, 9, 3, 5, 12, 12, 5, 3, 9 in each stanza.
l.2 WOKE: the subject of "woke" is "the morning"(l.5).
l.8 MYSELF: the object of "beckon(ing)" (l.5).
l.40 THE WEATHER TURNED AROUND: stanzas three and four have depicted a freak phenomenon – bright sunshine on the hill, but mist and rain below. Then in line 40 Thomas records an even greater phenomenon – the ability of memory (of childhood) to transform and transcend merely external weather. The difference is drawn between *external* delight ("marvel", l.38) and *inward* vision ("And I saw ... so clearly", l.46), between fancy ("tall tales", l.36) and real imagination.
l.42 THE OTHER AIR: that of vision and memory.
l.50 GREEN CHAPELS: woods.
l.51 TWICE TOLD: first lived through, and later remembered. There is the common pun on "told" = counted.

56 Holy Spring (November 1944)

Compare *Out of a war of wits* (p.6 above) from which this poem, over ten years later, seems to have sprung.
Waking from "a bed of love" to a world violently at war, the poet is forced to question in what way his work can remain affirmative and celebratory.
l.3 THAT IMMORTAL HOSPITAL: the "bed of love".
l.4 COUNTED BODY: because its days are numbered.

ll.8–9 The poet's involvement is not with the war's rights and wrongs, but with the fact that life ("light") is in any case borrowed time.

l.12 Presumably the sun makes him feel lonely because its confident reappearance contrasts with the poet's own feelings. "Holy maker" = poet.

l.18 PRODIGAL: because the rising sun has been away, wasting his beams elsewhere.

l.19 The sun symbolizes life itself. It will father new lives, almost as a revenge for the loss of those infants killed in the London raids.

ll.20–24 But the poet chooses instead to celebrate the anarchy and "upheaval", because (to paraphrase line 21) 'Since that turmoil is still with us, the only real certainty for the poet lies in standing alone and producing song from the midst of uncertainty'. "Toppling house" suggests the changing Zodiac.

57 The conversation of prayers (March 1945)

Compare Hardy's *On One Who Lived and Died Where He Was Born*. The curious music of this poem is produced by the mixture of end rhymes with carefully placed internal rhymes (e.g. stanza one: prayers-stairs-tears, said-bed-dead, love-move, room-whom). The way in which rhymes cross in the middle of lines is a structural reflection of the main theme – the crossing of two individual prayers.

l.1 CONVERSATION: a second meaning wittily implied is that of 'change': the situation of the man and the boy in the last stanza is the 'converse' of what it is in the first. A similar pun is made on the word "Turns" in line 6.

58 A Refusal to Mourn the Death, by Fire, of a Child in London (March 1945)

Compare Wordsworth's "A slumber did my spirit seal" and William Soutar's *The Children* (included in the 'Everyman Library' *Poems of Our Time*).

Unlike its negative title, the poem's tone is affirmative and positive in its evocation of the child's return into cosmic life. What it 'refuses' to do is fall into pious lament or propaganda.

ll.1–4 The subject of "tells" is "darkness". As the original darkness out of which life was created, it is described as 'making mankind', 'fathering bird, beast and flower', and 'humbling all'. The poem implies that the darkness will never again become a void.

ll.4–6 Note how these lines balance the negatives with positives: "*Tells* with *silence*", "the *last* light *breaking*", "the *still* hour ... of the sea *tumbling* in harness".

ll.8–9 "Zion" and "synagogue" make sacred the world of nature to which human life, in death, returns.

l.11 SALT SEED: tears.

l.12 SACKCLOTH (and ashes) are Old Testament signs of mourning.

l.14 MURDER: obscure, or make a travesty of.

l.15 THE MANKIND OF HER GOING: the 'naturalness' of her death (cf. Chaucer, "for no man can undo the law of kind [nature]"). In Shakespeare, the masculine word "mankind", when applied to a female, connotes cruelty ("the *man*kind of *her* going").

l.16 STATIONS OF THE BREATH: a play on 'stations of the cross'.

l.19 THE FIRST DEAD: the simplest meaning seems as strong as any other, i.e. the first mortals who ever died.

l.20 ROBED IN THE LONG FRIENDS: mixed with the "grains" and "veins" of others 'long' since dead. "Friends" suggests the kinship in death which life's hostilities denied.

l.21 THE DARK VEINS OF HER MOTHER: "mother" = *a* the girl's actual mother, *b* London (cf. "London's daughter", l.19), and *c* mother-earth. The last sense gives "veins" another meaning – that of mineral ore.

l.24 Though provocatively ambiguous, this last line promises, not resurrection, but continuing organic life. But Thomas possibly had in mind various references in Revelation (eg. xxi. 6–8) to a "second death".

59 This side of the truth (for Llewelyn) (March 1945)

Compare Yeats's *A Prayer for my Son*, Auden's *Lullaby* ("Lay your sleeping head, my love ..."), and Thomas's *In country sleep*.

Llewelyn was the poet's son, his first child, aged six when the poem was written. The poem claims that, however man himself may distinguish between Good and Bad, he does so in a completely neutral universe. Outside man, there is neither approval nor disapproval.

l.1 THIS SIDE OF THE TRUTH: this side of death, or this side of maturity.

l.13 GOOD AND BAD: this phrase is the subject of the next three main verbs ("Blow away", "Go crying", "Fly").

ll.23–28 In a completely physical world, death shows that Good and Bad have only an *imagined* reality. Like the "stars' blood", the "sun's tears", and the "moon's seed [sperm]", they are the result of man's tendency to anthropomorphize the 'elemental' universe.

l.29 WICKED WISH: the "wish" is the basic impulse towards creativity; only man's self-consciousness can make it appear "wicked".

l.36 LOVE: the word "love", in this context, draws all its meaning from its adjective, "unjudging".

60 A Winter's Tale (March 1945)

As a phrase, "a winter's tale" traditionally refers to a story told, not for its significance, but for the more trivial aim of whiling away a winter evening. Though Thomas's poem owes nothing important to

Shakespeare's *The Winter's Tale*, both titles heighten (by first denying) the tragic proportions of the stories they introduce. Such titles also warn us that the tales will not be completely realistic ones.

It seems clear that the "she-bird" embodies mainly the regenerative power of sexual love, delivering the man from the winter world of loneliness, old age, and the seasons.

The poem's stanzas are apportioned as follows: *Stanzas 1–2* (Present tense) the in-coming twilight carries with it a story associated with the described landscape. *Stanzas 3–11* (Past tense) the tale itself starts being told. *Stanzas 12–13* (Present tense) an address to the reader, saying that all previous life seems reborn in the landscape. *Stanza 14* (Past tense) one stanza developing the tale itself: the "she-bird" appears. *Stanzas 15–16* (Present tense) another address to the reader, like stanzas twelve-thirteen. *Stanzas 17–22* (Past tense) the tale itself continued: the man follows the "she-bird". *Stanzas 23–24* (Present tense) showing the vision of past life dying back into the landscape. *Stanzas 25–26* (Past tense) the culmination of the tale itself: the "she-bird" and the man 'die' in sexual union, but phoenix-like arise to a new life.

l.29 THE QUICK OF NIGHT: a reversal of 'the dead of night'.

ll.42–43 Water turned into snowflakes is compared to manna, the 'bread' with which God fed the hungry Israelites; thus the "high corn" and the "harvest" melting on the birds' tongues are the falling snow itself.

ll.48–50 Like a "lost believer" or Satan ("the hurled outcast of light"), he seeks a divine rebirth ("inhuman cradle").

ll.54–55 He prays that the product of his union with the "engulfing bride" will not, like "seed" or "flesh", be subject to death.

l.121 FOR THE BIRD LAY BEDDED …: the sense runs on, not from the previous stanza, but from line 110, and explains how "the tale ended".

61 In my craft or sullen art (September 1945)

Compare Yeats's *Sailing to Byzantium*.

A general comment in an essay by W. H. Auden seems a good approximation to the theme of this poem: "The impulse to create a work of art is felt when, in certain persons, the passive awe provoked by sacred beings or events is transformed into a desire to express that awe in a rite of worship or homage … nothing is expected in return."

Broken only in line 14, the basic pattern in each stanza is a series of 7-syllable lines ending in a final line of 6.

l.1 CRAFT OR SULLEN ART: Thomas viewed his poetry generally as a difficult *craft*. If it is an *art* at all, it is an art made "sullen" ('morose', 'gloomy') by that difficulty. But "sullen" here also means 'solitary', 'lonely'.

l.5 Embracing lovers hold all that concerns them in their arms.

l.6 SINGING LIGHT: the light of lamp or moon by which the poet 'sings'.

(The lamp itself might also be thought of as making a noise.)

ll.8-9 Cheap popularity (and financial reward) earned by flashy posturing.

IVORY also links with the word "towering" later (line 15) to suggest the 'ivory tower'– the usual image for art's sometimes unrealistic aloofness from ordinary human affairs.

ll.10-11 The poet's rewards are the same as those of the lovers – relationship, love, commitment to human limitations.

l.14 SPINDRIFT: light spray blown off the sea, suggesting here the impermanence of poetry.

l.15 TOWERING DEAD: either those in 'ivory towers', dead to the world of ordinary life; or those dead men with "towering" reputations already honoured by the "nightingales and psalms" of life and literature.

62 Fern Hill (September 1945)

Compare Henry Vaughan's *The Retreate*, Wordsworth's *Ode: Intimations of Immortality*, Philip Larkin's *I Remember, I Remember*, John Clare's *Remembrances* and Thomas's different treatment of the same farm in the first story of his *Portrait of the Artist as a Young Dog*.

Fern Hill is a farm just outside Carmarthen. Thomas spent many childhood holidays there at a time when it was the home of Ann Jones, the aunt commemorated in *After the funeral*. In a letter, Thomas said of *Fern Hill* that "it's a poem for evening and tears".

Only lines 6 and 52 break the syllabic count of 14, 14, 9, 6, 9, 14, 14 in the first seven lines of each stanza. And even the 7, 9, 7, 9, 9, 6; 9, 6, 9, 6, 7, 9 of the two final lines in each stanza would seem to have a pattern. Equally consistent is the use of assonance (vowel repetition) instead of rhymes at the line-endings (e.g. boughs-towns, green-leaves, starry-barley, climb-eyes-light).

l.3 DINGLE: a small wooded valley.

l.4 HAIL AND CLIMB suggests stopping the hay-waggon and climbing aboard.

l.9 WINDFALL: prematurely fallen. A literal picture of light on early-fallen apples. "Windfall" also carries connotations of good luck.

ll.13-14 A good example of how the syntax allows several meanings at once: Time let him play and be golden; Time let him play and live ("be"); and Time let him play and left him alone ("let me ...be").

l.20 TUNES FROM THE CHIMNEYS: smoke wafted on the air.

ll.20-22 Notice the covert suggestion of the four elements – air, water, fire, earth.

FIRE GREEN AS GRASS: fire as intense as grass is green. Cf. "bonfire green" in D.H. Lawrence's poem *The Enkindled Spring*.

ll.24-29 The childlike notion that, while the boy is asleep, the farm does not exist; that it exists in and for his own consciousness.

l.30 MAIDEN: by not mentioning Eve by name, the poet helps the idea that it was all his own (Adam's) world.

l.47 BY THE SHADOW OF MY HAND: hidden in the syntax is the common expression "take me ... by the ... hand". "Shadow", however, indicates the intangible touch of Time.

l.51 CHILDLESS LAND: "childless" because the child has grown up.

l.53 HELD: because of "chains" in the next line, "held" means 'chained'; but because of "mercy" in the previous line, it also suggests 'cradled', 'supported'.

63 On A Wedding Anniversary (September 1945)

An earlier published version of this poem was longer and different in effect. But it confirms the fact that the setting is that of the wartime air-raids. With one exception, the syllabic count is 6, 10, 7, 7.

l.3 THREE YEARS: the earlier version (published January 1941) had been written close to the third anniversary (11 July 1940) of Thomas's own marriage.

l.6 LOVE AND HIS PATIENTS: the horror of the bombing drives the man and wife mad. Love itself is seen as a demented asylum warder. Previously "in tune" (l.3), they now "roar on a chain".

ll.7–8 CRATER/CARRYING CLOUD: a cloud-like formation of falling bombs, which will cause the crater; or the cloud in which the aeroplane is flying.

l.9 THE WRONG RAIN: falling bombs. Play on 'right as rain'.

l.10 "They come together" in the sense that they are finally made one in instantaneous death. In which case "parted" probably means 'made into separate individuals'. Formerly separate individuals, the violence of the bombs makes their bodies inseparable (notice the singular nouns which follow – "their *heart,* "their *brain*").

64 In Country Sleep (April–July 1947)

Compare Coleridge's *Frost at Midnight* and Yeats's *A Prayer for My Daughter.*
The poet addresses his sleeping daughter, urging her not to fear what children usually fear, the fantastic figures of fairy tales, nursery rhymes, and superstition. The countryside which is the source of these imagined characters is, itself, benign and safe. The only figure to fear is the Thief – Time, Experience, but mainly Death. And yet the very certainty of his coming shows he is part of the natural scheme of things. Safety from this real fear comes in an awareness of that planned pattern.

l.16 MY RIDER: his daughter, "riding" the world of dreams.

l.38 THE THIEF: image from the Bible, e.g. 2 Peter, iii. 10: "But the day of the Lord will come as a thief in the night."

l.95 WOUND: in the poem "wound" seems to stand for 'heart'.

l.96 From this line onwards, the poet concentrates on words which suggest purpose and control: "designed", "truly", "ruly", "surely", "ship shape" etc.

ll.99–106 The manuscripts at the Humanities Research Centre, University of Texas, contain paraphrases of these lines as follows: "If you believe (and fear) that every night, night without end, the Thief comes to try to steal your faith that every night he comes to steal your faith that your faith is there – then you will wake with your faith steadfast and deathless.

If you are innocent of the Thief, you are in danger. If you are innocent of the loss of faith, you cannot be faithful. If you do not know the Thief as well as you know God, then you do not know God well. Christian looked through a hole in the floor of heaven and saw hell. You must look through faith, and see disbelief."

65 Over Sir John's hill (May–August 1949)

Compare Hopkins's *The Windhover* and Ted Hughes's *The Hawk in the Rain.*

Sir John's Hill overlooks the estuary in Laugharne.

l.2 THE HAWK ON FIRE HANGS STILL: "on fire" and "hangs" are the start of two main lines of imagery. Thus "on fire" (dynamic in action and reflecting the sun) yields "rays", "fiery", "flash" (twice), "on fire", "fuse", "flames" etc.; and "hangs" yields images of guilt, execution, and judgment – "hoisted", "drop", "gallows", "tyburn", "noosed", "black cap", "just hill", "halter" etc. Thomas, as "young Aesop" (l.35), witnesses the hierarchy of natural death: the hawk kills the sparrows, but is itself "noosed".

ll.21–2 Cf. "John Ostler, go fetch me a duckling or two;/Cry Dilly, dilly, dilly, dilly, come and be killed" in the nursery song *Mrs Bond.*

l.33 WE: the poet and the heron.

l.51 IN THE TEAR OF THE TOWY: Thomas stressed that he meant "tear" as in *tare*, not as in *tier* (ie. the heron is fishing in a 'torn-off' section of the river). The word is distantly echoed in the later phrase "*wear*-willow". The Towy is one of two rivers running into the estuary at Laugharne.

l.58 GRAVE: engrave.

66 In the White Giant's Thigh (November 1949)

Compare Thomas Hardy's *In Front of the Landscape.*

The poet walks over a "high chalk hill" (the White Giant of the title) at night, and imagines the former lives of the childless women lying buried there, and the survival of their longings even in death. There is, in fact, a white giant figure carved in chalk, associated with fertility superstition, at Cerne Abbas, Dorset, near where the family often stayed with Caitlin's mother – at Blashford in Hampshire.

A regular structure of fifteen rhymed quatrains is intentionally obscured by irregular layout.

l.1 RIVERS: presumably rivers of blood in the curlews' throats.

l.14 WAINS: waggons.

l.17 LIGHTED SHAPES OF FAITH: the stars.

l.29 HAWED: overgrown with wild thorn.

l.37 GAMBO: a common word in Wales for a haycart.

l.39 SHIPPEN: cowshed.

l.59 FOR EVER MERIDIAN: for ever at highest pitch or in their prime.

67 Lament (March 1951)

Compare Yeats's *The Wild Old Wicked Man*, and Louis MacNeice's *The Libertine*.

Of all the poems which Thomas included in his *Collected Poems* in 1952, this is the one which has the clearest affinities with the comic gusto of the poet's prose works and with some of the characterization in *Under Milk Wood*.

l.12 COAL BLACK: this phrase, present in each stanza, is one of the remaining signs that in an early version in the Humanities Research Centre Library, University of Texas, the poem's title had been "The Miner's Lament". Images such as "the moon shaft slag" and "the skinbare pit" disappeared from the poem, but "black spit", "ram rod", "wick" etc. still faintly reflect its earlier 'mining' idiom.

68 Do not go gentle into that good night (March 1951)

Compare Thomas's unfinished *Elegy* and William Empson's *To an Old Lady*.

Addressed to the poet's father as he approached blindness and death. The relevant aspect of the relationship was Thomas's profound respect for his father's uncompromising independence of mind, now tamed by illness. In the face of strong emotion, the poet sets himself the task of mastering it in the difficult form of the villanelle. Five tercets are followed by a quatrain, with the first and last line of the first stanza repeated alternately as the last line of subsequent stanzas and gathered into a couplet at the end of the quatrain. And all this on only two rhymes.

The poem has strong echoes of Yeats's favourite words – "rage", "gay" and "blaze" – and the middle four stanzas, describing the common approach to death of four different types of men, recall the fifth section of Yeats's *Nineteen Hundred and Nineteen*.

l.5 HAD FORKED NO LIGHTNING: had given and brought no revelation. Probably an echo of Shakespeare: "How oft when men are at the point of death/ Have they been merry! which their keepers call/A lightning before death"(*Romeo and Juliet* V, 3, 88–90).

l.8 IN A GREEN BAY: in a friendly world.

l.14 GAY: the same idea as Yeats's "tragic gaiety" – an exulting acceptance of life's tragedies, contrasted with the previous glum pessimism of the "grave men".

l.16 ON THE SAD HEIGHT: with echoes of King Lear and Gloucester in Shakespeare's play. Also, Thomas did not deny a suggestion that Vernon Watkins once made to him, that the image might owe something to Kierkegaard hearing of his father standing on a high hill, cursing God.

69 Poem on his Birthday (Autumn 1949–Summer 1951)

Compare D. H. Lawrence's *The Ship of Death*.

The poem owes most of its imagery and atmosphere to its location in Laugharne. The "house on stilts" (l.4) is either the Boat House where the poet lived or the nearby shed where he did most of his writing at this time. He may have begun the poem as early as October 1949 if line 8 – "His driftwood thirty-fifth wind turned age" – is intended literally. A significant dimension in the poem's imagery ("hammer flame", "rocketing wind" etc) is the poet's apprehension regarding the threat of a Third (atomic) World War. Thomas highlighted as much in a summary of the poem given to Bill Read: "he, who is progressing, afraid, to his own fiery end in the cloud of an atomic explosion knows that, out at sea, animals who attack and eat other sea animals are tasting the flesh of their own death ... His death lurks for him, and for all, in the next lunatic war."

With only one exception, the lines of each stanza alternate between 6 and 9 syllables. Assonance (agreement of vowels) replaces rhyme, and every stanza after the first has the same assonance-scheme.

l.23 WYNDS: a dialect word for 'alleys'.

l.38 ANGELUS: literally, a Catholic devotional exercise commemorating the Incarnation.

ll.42–45 The immediate future ("tomorrow") may have its cage torn open by "terror" (another war); but the ultimate future ("the dark") will be freed by love in death. What Thomas imagines from here on is not a Christian heaven, but a continuing process deprived of terror and uncertainty.

l.85 NIMBUS: bright cloud or halo.

70 Elegy

Compare Thomas's *Do not go gentle into that good night*.

The poet had been working on this elegy to his father (died 16 December 1952) right up to his departure on his last trip to America in the autumn of 1953, but it was left unfinished at the poet's death in America that November. A notebook in the Humanities Research Centre, University of Texas, contains drafts of lines for the poem, along with 33 numbered sheets. On sheet 2 is entered the poem as printed here, titled 'Elegy', and representing the stage towards which the draft materials had so far led. On sheet 30, Thomas wrote down his original thoughts for the poem: *(1) Although he was too proud to die, he did die, blind, in the most agonizing way but he did not flinch from death & was brave in his pride. (2) In his innocence, & thinking he was God-hating, he never knew that what he was was: an old kind man in his burning pride. (3) Now he will not leave my side, though he is dead. (4) His mother said that as a baby he never cried; nor did he, as an old man; he just cried to his secret wound & his blindness, never aloud.*

SUGGESTIONS FOR FURTHER READING

(*Except where otherwise stated, the publishers are Dent*)

The standard biographies are *The Life of Dylan Thomas* (1965) by Constantine FitzGibbon, who had the advantage of being a friend and contemporary during the London years, and *Dylan Thomas* (Hodder and Stoughton, 1977) by Paul Ferris, a product of the Swansea of the next generation after Thomas's. Because of especially the Welsh background that moulded it, the poet's 'life' is a meaningful starting-point. But because of the life's bohemian indiscretions it also raises W.B. Yeats's famous conundrum – do we look for "perfection of the life or of the work"? The careless, untidy life is more specifically related to the careful, almost care-worn, work in a biography of smaller compass such as John Ackerman's *Welsh Dylan* (John Jones, 1979) and in the excellent account of the poet's friendship with Vernon Watkins in Gwen Watkins's *Portrait of a Friend* (Gomer, 1983). Vivid correlations between the life and the work, via detailed discussions of individual poems, are revealed also in *Letters to Vernon Watkins*, edited by the recipient (Faber/Dent, 1957). Constantine FitzGibbon's edition of the *Selected Letters* (1966) has been superseded by Paul Ferris's *The Collected Letters* (1985). The early letters to Pamela Hansford Johnson are probably the best introduction to the personality of the young man.

The definitive edition of the Collected Poems is *Dylan Thomas: Collected Poems 1934–1953*, edited by Walford Davies and Ralph Maud (1988), and an important volume for further study of the poetry is Ralph Maud's edition of *The Notebook Poems 1930–1934* (1989).

The comic vision of the prose works, which have in some ways been undervalued, supplements the more sombre vision of the poetry, and there are important parallels between prose and poetry in terms of stylistic development. Accordingly, the volumes recommended here are given in the broad chronological order of the prose works that they contain. The early short stories are included mainly in *A Prospect of the Sea*, edited by Daniel Jones (1955) but others will be found in *Dylan Thomas: Early Prose Writings*, edited by Walford Davies (1971). The autobiographical material of the middle-period short stories in *Portrait of the Artist as a Young Dog* (1940) extended naturally into the unfinished 'novel' *Adventures in the Skin Trade* (Putnam 1955). Good examples of the film scripts which Thomas was writing around 1944 would be *Twenty Years A-Growing* (1964) and *The Doctor and the Devils* (1953). A collection *Dylan Thomas: The Filmscripts* (1995) has been edited by John Ackerman and the radio broadcasts that helped make the poet a household name between 1943 and 1953 have been edited by Ralph Maud as *Dylan Thomas: The Broadcasts* (1991). His work in film and broadcasts of course helped prepare him for the writing of his radio 'play for voices' *Under Milk Wood*, the definitive edition of which has been edited by Walford Davies and Ralph Maud (1995).

Of the numerous critical studies, one offering a general overview might be selected first. The interest of Henry Treece's *Dylan Thomas: 'Dog Among the Fairies'* (1949; revised edition, Ernest Benn, 1956) is its status as the earliest attempt to evaluate the full achievement. Also early was Derek Stanford's survey of the career in *Dylan Thomas* (Neville Spearman 1954 – reissued 1964). Jacob Korg's *Dylan Thomas* (Twayne, 1965) is a lucid and more detailed overview. John Ackerman's *Dylan Thomas: His Life and Work* (1964 – reissued Macmillan, 1991), the chapter on Dylan Thomas in Glyn Jones's *The Dragon Has Two Tongues* (1968), the two essays on Thomas in Roland Mathias's *A Ride Through the Wood: Essays on Anglo-Welsh Literature* (Poetry Wales Press, 1985) and Walford Davies's *Dylan Thomas* (University of Wales Press 1972 – reissued 1990) develop particularly the Welsh background. John Ackerman's *A Dylan Thomas Companion* (Macmillan, 1991) is a capacious treatment of the complete career.

Scholarly and helpful in its approach to problems of detail and technique, Ralph Maud's *Entrances to Dylan Thomas' Poetry* (Scorpion Press, 1963) also contains a valuable 'Chronology of Composition', and William T. Moynihan's *The Craft and Art of Dylan Thomas* (Oxford University Press, 1966) is a sensitive discussion of the poet's auditory, rhetorical, and metaphorical techniques. Two outstanding analysts of Thomas's use of language are: John Bayley in *The Romantic Survival* (Constable and Oxford University Press, 1957) and Winifred Nowottny in *The Language Poets Use* (Athlone Press, 1962). The 'Twentieth Century Views' volume on Thomas, edited by C.B. Cox (Prentice-Hall, 1966) is a balanced selection from some of the most interesting criticism to that date, and a wide variety of later critical approaches and assessments is reflected in the specially commissioned essays of *Dylan Thomas: New Critical Essays*, edited by Walford Davies (1972) and *Dylan Thomas: Craft or Sullen Art*, edited by Alan Bold (Vision Press,

1990). In tackling the most immediate difficulties of individual poems, the reader may find useful the poem-by-poem format of W.Y. Tindall's *A Reader's Guide to Dylan Thomas* (Thames and Hudson, 1962), Clark Emery's *The World of Dylan Thomas* (1962 – reissued Dent 1971), and Walford Davies's *Dylan Thomas* (Open University Press, 1986).

Full bibliographical guidance is available in Ralph Maud's *Dylan Thomas in Print* (1972) and Georg M.A. Gaston's *Dylan Thomas: A Reference Guide* (1987).

INDEX OF TITLES AND FIRST LINES

Titles of poems are in *italics*.
Where the first line of a poem is exactly the same as the title, it is not repeated.

POETRY
IN EVERYMAN